SMALL TOWN HO

DUKE DIERCKS

Slog Press
Sandpoint, Idaho

Duke Diercks/Slog Press
401 Lake St.
Sandpoint, Idaho/83864
www.smalltownho.com

Publisher's Note: This is a memoir. As such, it relies on the
author's memory, and should not be taken as fact. Names,
characters, and places have been changed. Locales and public
names are sometimes used for atmospheric purposes.

Book Layout ©2013 BookDesignTemplates.com

Ordering Information:
Quantity sales. Special discounts are available on quantity purchases by corporations, associations, and others. For details,
contact the "Special Sales Department" at the address above.

Book Title/ Author Name. -- 1st ed.
ISBN 978-0-6926322-3-9

For Monique Gallegos Diekroeger
The stalker without whom this book would never have happened

···

ONE

GO SMALL OR GO HOME

I blame my adulthood on two people.

Bingo.

Joseph Campbell and Robert Frost. To be fair and accurate, I do not blame my entire adulthood on these two men; rather, I blame them solely for the decisions I've made. Robert Frost encouraged me to take the road less traveled. Joe Campbell encouraged me to follow my bliss. Frost neglected to mention, perhaps due to poetic confines, that some roads have potholes so there may be a very good reason that people avoid them. Mr. Campbell left out the part that if your particular bliss entails long hours and little pay, perhaps bliss might be better off *purchased*. They should not shoulder the blame by themselves. My wife, Kim, is also complicit, if only as a willing accomplice.

All three weighed heavily on our decision to uproot our family that has only lived in cities—and warm ones, at that—and move to the North Idaho Panhandle. That is correct: two college-educated adults made such a fantastically ignorant decision, and brought their three children along for the ride. The added bonus? This would be the second cross-country move for our family within five years. The first move came after a dozen years in the California Bay Area, and the second came after only three years in Austin, Texas.

We wound up in the Texas capital thanks to the California Department of Motor Vehicles. I was there to renew my driver's license. While I did not delude myself that this was going to be a painless exercise, I was cautiously optimistic for two reasons. First, I had made what the DMV euphemistically refers to as an "appointment," a new customer service initiative for them at the time. Second, the appointment was mid-morning, well after rush hour. However, California didn't really have a *rush hour* any more: any part of the day on the freeway was a shit storm. And this was the California DMV, where time stands still. After spending an hour on the 101 freeway to trudge only a few miles, I arrived to find several hundred of California's finest citizens had also booked an appointment at that time. As I aged in line, focusing simultaneously on the backs of people in front of me blocking access to the Promised Land, and the department clerks directing this symphony, a thought dropped from the ether like an anvil in an old Warner Bros. cartoon: *We need to get out of here. Out of here, out of this city, and out of this state.* I flipped open the black brick that was my cellular phone, called Kim, and we agreed that yes, my experience that morning was sufficient cause to move.

Of course that's silly. The DMV was not the

reason we moved to Austin. It was just the trigger that started our thought process. No, the real reason we picked Austin is because we really liked a hotel there. Our decision-making was as scientific and logical as that—we moved our growing family thousands of miles because we enjoyed staying in the Austin Four Seasons Hotel. Two things about that statement jump out at me now: it is amazing to me how *little* thought we've given to life-changing decisions yet how *much* thought to what we are going to have for dinner, and it is astounding how logical our thought process seemed at the time.

Texas also was an enticing option because for me, it was home. I grew up in Houston, and while I would not move back to that swamp, despite my fond memories, Texas itself had a magnetic pull. For Kim, whose father is ex-military and whose family moved more times than most people change socks, moving anywhere wasn't that big a deal. She'd had no real home other than California, and was game for most anything. Ultimately we decided that moving to Texas from the Bay Area was in the cards only if one of us could land a job before we actually left. We were at least that rational. Quick employment for me was going to be dicey, since in California I had followed the aforementioned Mr. Campbell's advice and followed my bliss into the restaurant business. However, a few years running a small restaurant with a friend had burned me out, and I wanted to switch careers. So, even though I was optimistic, the smart money was on my wife.

Enter: Mrs. Magoo.

I refer to my wife as Mrs. Magoo in reference to that golden oldie of a cartoon that I used to watch at YMCA day camp in Houston, on an old-timey 8mm projector. The main character, Mr. Magoo, is horribly myopic, and would walk perilously close to fatal accidents only to be rescued at the last minute. Obviously it's a cartoon, so there's not much plot, but a typical episode went something like this: Mr. Magoo is walking across skyscraper girders. Never mind how he got up there. He is coming to the end of the girder. What will happen? Why, another steel beam magically appears via a crane that was nowhere to be found only seconds earlier. And, in the nick of time, he keeps walking.

And so it is with my wife.

Her girders are career opportunities. As one job or career ends, another job comes along by providence, or the situation itself has a silver lining. I witnessed it time and again in the early stages of her career. She likes to say she puts positive thoughts and requests out to the universe and then just waits for good things to happen. I find that type of subversive thinking deprives you of a lot of needless worry. Mrs. Magoo's girder arrived on a quick trip we took to Austin to get the lay of the land and say hello to some friends I had gone to high school with, and who were going to house us until we could find an apartment. During the visit, she stopped by the local headhunting office specializing in Certified Public Accountants. (After college, Kim had taken the road *well-*

traveled, one ripe with career opportunities: she was a CPA.) She met with the regional director, they hit it off, and she was offered a job on the spot—not one as a CPA, but as a corporate recruiter. I balanced my annoyance with husbandly pride. The move was on.

The fact that Kim landed a job first didn't just mean that Austin was going to be a reality, it also meant that I had to care for the kids—at least until I could find gainful employment and we could then plop them into day care. Our days were filled with the Teletubbies and Sesame Street. We had regular bath times and trips to the park. On rainy days we built forts constructed of overturned chairs abutting tables, with blankets stretched over the top. We made swords, shields, and helmets from an entire box of aluminum foil. It is, they say, the most difficult yet rewarding job in the world.

I hated it.

"They" never mentioned that it is mind-numbingly boring. Not boring in the classic sense. No, there is always something going on. The little ones are spilling something, or knocking each other down, or asking "why" after your every utterance. It is boring in the sense that you simply don't have thoughts other than survival. No deep thinking, just counting down the clock until nap time. And with two kids, heaven forbid one of them is not tired. There is also no verbal engagement using more than 100 words of your vocabulary. In a sense it is Twitter come to horrible life.

At first, my thoughts were that I was doing something wrong. After all, women happily sign on to this lifestyle all the time. However, mothers also tend to bond with each other at the park and strike up conversations, using their adult vocabularies and making play dates to share the burden. When I tried that, despite having toddlers in tow, those same mothers moved to the other side of the park, or left altogether. Then my thoughts turned to wonder. I wondered, *How can you love two little beings so much and at the same time entertain the thought of slipping them some Benadryl in their sippy cups?*

I was not cut out for it. No wonder I was such an asshole when my wife got home.

Eighteen months into our relocation we became aware that indeed we were *not* living in a hotel. We were, in fact, living in a "custom home" in a new development on the outskirts of the city, at least technically still a part of Austin. It was a cookie cutter home sitting on a large, treeless lot that, in the middle of summer, looked like a lunar landscape. We moved there after our apartment became too small to house us and our two young sons, apparent after a very brief conversation.

Kim came home one night and, as usual, I was waging a dinner battle involving Cheerios, Vienna sausages, and something green. She was acting weird. Jittery. Nervous. My wife is not the devious kind, and rarely suspicious. In fact she is the easiest person on the planet for whom to plan a surprise party. She simply does not think about anything other than the task at hand. So it was with some telekinetic husbandly intuition that I knew something was wrong. And just like that, I *knew*.

"You're pregnant."

Red bloomed from the top of her head to the base of her neck. Bullseye.

"Fuck!"

My mother-in-law's response, when we broke the news, was only marginally better than my own: "OH NO! Aggggh! What are you doing to her?!"

We also realized that our new house was not a hotel when our days were spent not ordering cocktails by the pool, but rather cold-calling. Kim had been doing it for a while at this point, and I was just starting, thanks to my new job working for my father's company. He'd founded JanSteam about a dozen or so years earlier. JanSteam sells small steam cleaners to hotels, food service businesses, and other hospitality establishments. At the time, though, before infomercials touted the benefits of steam, we sold to anyone who would listen. And often, that was not many people, and if they would listen, when they heard the price they would look at you like you were Wilbur the talking horse: a little funny and totally unbelievable.

Since the product often required a demonstration to convince someone to fork over upwards of a thousand dollars, we had to set up demonstration appointments, pre-Internet, over the phone. My days largely consisted of staring at the phone—and I mean this quite literally, *staring at the phone*—getting up the nerve to make a cold call. I became Cindy Brady staring at the TV monitor on the Brady Bunch. It's *Baton Rouge* Cindy, *Baton Rouge*. I simply could not pick up the phone and make appointments, and was not much better doing it in person. At the time, we didn't have the mercy killing of voice mail. No, in the good old days we got the opportunity of waiting to hear that awful pause when they realized not only that they don't know you, but also that they couldn't give two shits if you live or die. Awful.

Evenings, after the kids were fed and put to bed, we would commiserate about our days. While not ecstatic, Kim was not as miserable as I was for a variety of reasons. First, she has a remarkable ability to buy into a plan once you show her the strategy and her place in it. Also, her job had proven to be quite lucrative. Even though she was making literally hundreds of calls a day, her office had a social atmosphere, while I was working from home without anyone to talk to. And in stark contrast to my customer base, Kim was reaching out to high-level finance types, whereas I was reaching out to 17-year-old fast food assistant managers, hoping to talk to them about a better way to clean the grout in their johns.

Our growing sense of malaise subtly presented itself on our Friday poker nights. This was not a formal group of players joined around a green felt table with colored chips, cigars and beer. No, this was just Kim and me hunkered over our Pottery Barn table with glasses of chardonnay after we had put the boys to bed. Looking for an alternative to TV, I had offered up the idea of playing poker, probably with some ulterior motive of having it degenerate into strip poker. When my wife told me she had no idea how to play, my eyes lit up. Our problem was betting. We played with paper clips, so Kim simply went "all in" every time since they had no value. Actual money was no better; we didn't have a lot in the first place, and we were, in essence, playing with the same pot. We needed an alternative that had real value, so I tore up some pieces of paper and scribbled on them "favors." I didn't categorize them like the old Disney ride coupon books; the actual bets would take care of what was an "E" ticket and what was a teacup ride. The bets included:

- A backrub
- No laundry duties
- A sexual favor of the other's choice
- A free afternoon
- Sleeping in
- Reading bedtime stories

We knew we were in a bit of a rut when on a regular basis the royal flush of a bet—the E ticket—was "sleeping in," a wager that just surpassed "a day to do whatever I want." It wasn't necessarily that these ranked so high; any parent of toddlers dreams about these. It's that the sexual favors and back rubs were opening bets, no better than an ante.

So, three years into our relocation, spoken and unspoken feelings started to simmer. We started talking about the lack of support and the feeling that we were just treading water. At my behest, we had gone home. Although we weren't aware of it at the time, we were about to go small.

TWO

···

WESTWARD HO! BUT WHERE?

I blame our decision to move to Idaho on an event that took place on September 11, 2001.

Bingo.

The food processing trade show I was attending in Las Vegas.

I was there not as an attendee, but rather as an exhibitor. In addition to cold calls, in the nascent days of the Internet trade shows were a major method JanSteam had of obtaining sales leads and introducing our steam cleaners to the throngs of ready buyers. In the ideal-world scenario, trade shows allow sellers to introduce buyers to exciting new products and exchange ideas and solutions. In the real-world scenario, sellers anxiously await buyers, hoping to catch their attention as they walk down a narrow strip of garishly colored low-nap shag carpeting. Cautious buyers or convention visitors do their best not to make eye contact or show interest, lest the salesmen engage. It was this very uncomfortable *pasodoble* that inspired my father to develop JanSteam's "jewelry cleaning routine" that, although surely attracting a crowd, in most cases had nothing whatsoever to do with the nature of the trade show we were attending. It went something like this:

"Sir! Sir! May I clean your watch for you?"

A puzzled look from "Sir" ensues. He is confused; this is not a jewelry trade show. This is a pest control convention.

"Miss! Miss! May I clean your rings? Your bracelet?"

If sir or madam were brave enough to hand over their jewelry to us, perfect strangers, we would then zap their items with dry steam and clean all of the hard-to-reach nooks and crannies. It worked remarkably well, both the cleaning and attracting visitors. When watches were particularly dirty, the line was, "My, sir/miss, look at all the sins I'm burning off!" Inevitably a crowd would gather, since people really are interested in getting their jewelry cleaned for free—especially when they are trapped at a soul-sucking, three-day trade show about packaging equipment or durable medical goods. Once the crowd formed, my father, or my sister, or anyone with a sales gift for gab (unlike me) would pounce:

Dad: "I always say that having a clean bathroom with dirty grout, or a beautiful factory with state-of-the-art equipment but dirty floor drains is like a beautiful woman with large bosoms in a low-cut dress who has dirty fingernails! Yessir."

Or, when asked about the warranty on one of our steam cleaners, my sister: "Well, all I can tell you is that mine has lasted longer than any of my husbands!" And we were off to the races.

As the newly appointed JanSteam Southwest Regional Manager with a staff of zero, I was alone in our booth at the trade show that morning, my index finger on the steam toggle, doing my level best to swallow down my embarrassment and launch into the spiel. Around the room, there was a murmur amongst the visitors and the exhibitors that felt strange. It wasn't the normal sales banter. The company in the booth next to mine had brought a television to display product videos; when they switched it over to live TV, our corner of the convention hall saw the reason for the murmurs: the second plane had impaled the second tower of the World Trade Center.

For the rest of the day, with even Sin City in turmoil, not one person visited the show. I left the next morning, picking up the rental car that I had reserved weeks prior from the airport parking lot. It was the only car left in the entire lot—an eerie sight. Instead of driving back to Los Angeles to do a scheduled demonstration and then catch a flight home, I decided to put Las Vegas, whose overt American excess I was certain would make a high-value terrorist target, in my rearview mirror but in the other direction. I drove all the way back to Texas. That drive, much of it through miles of scrub, gave me time to think. *What am I doing? What are we doing?* Once home, Kim and I started to think seriously about our situation and about moving.

Here's what we thought about. We lived in my old state, but in a new city. The few old friends I had there had new friends. We knew one family in our subdivision and, frankly, wore out our welcome with them. They would probably not admit it, but towards the end they were avoiding us. We had a grand total of one "date night" and one babysitter in three years. We had no family close by. And it was hot enough to melt paint on most summer days. We thought about moving.

But where? For this discussion we were a tad bit more analytical about where and what, at least on the surface, we were looking for. We knew one thing: we wanted to get back to the western US. Whereas there are beautiful spots in this land of ours, the West is majestic. It also is not humid. It also is not home to school-bus-sized roaches that can fly, and not particularly well. We thought about California again, but only briefly. If anything, it had become more crowded and expensive than when we last lived there. We thought about Portland. But they have a cute expression in Portland: "It's not raining if you can still see Mt. Hood." Cute, but this translates into "it rains so much here that we create jokes about how much it rains here." Uh, no. Seattle? Great city, but it rains more than Portland, and it has some of the highest home prices in the country as well as some of the worst traffic. No.

We also knew that with three boys under the age of six, we needed some support, if only in the form of a babysitter. I knew that I wanted at some point to get back into the restaurant business since food was a nagging obsession. We both wanted a slower pace, since the crowds and traffic that encouraged our move from California had followed us to Austin.

I'm not sure if Kim's parents suggested it, or if we thought of it first, but eventually Sandpoint, Idaho entered the conversation. Kim's dad, a retired U.S. Marine Colonel, and her mom, a naturalized Swede, retired to the North Idaho Panhandle in 1993, to Sandpoint. The impetus? They saw it in a brochure. They didn't know a single soul there, they just saw it in a brochure. Not too far a jump from our relocating to a city because we liked a hotel. Maybe that's where half of our decision-making genius comes from. But Sandpoint had fit all of their criteria: a water feature (mountain lake), a local ski mountain, an international airport close by, and white supremacists.

Kidding on that last part—that was not part of the criteria, just a bonus.

Kidding again.

I am also *sort of* kidding about the international airport thing. It's true: Spokane Airport is "international." I guess since technically GEG has flights to Canada, maybe once a day, it is an international airport in the way a podiatrist is a doctor. My in-laws raved about the place, except for the insanely long winters. Actually, my father-in-law loved those. He skied every single winter day, unless it was raining, so winters were a snap. We had visited her parents two or three times for Christmas during our California years. It was the place we *swore* we'd never be able to live. The place that, at the time, had one Main Street, maybe six restaurants and most of them mediocre, and whose only national claim to fame was the Ruby Ridge massacre. (To be fair, that was 45 minutes away near Naples, Idaho.) The place was situated in an area that quaintly called itself the "Inland Northwest." ("The Pacific Northwest" was already taken and the Pacific is eight hours away.) The place that was a six-hour drive from a real city. Sorry Spokane. The place where, during one visit, when trying to find avocados at the grocery store in the dead of winter, we noticed customers, heads down against the wind, plowing their carts through inches of slush, and thought, "People live here?"

Enter: The Power of Rationalization.

"But," we said.

"But," we said, "since we first visited, the Internet was born. Now any newspaper is a click away. "But," we said, "with satellite TV we will have the same number of channels in Sandpoint or a city." "But," we said, "we will have built-in babysitters! We can go out on the town on occasion." Although seriously, how often did we dine out now that we had kids? Our lives consisted of an endless loop of Cheerios, the park, diapers and formula.

"But," we said, "it would be nice to see natural beauty that is hard to match anywhere, instead of miles of highways and strip malls." We thought the kids would walk to school, we wouldn't worry about abductors, and Kim already had plans to have lunch with her mother every week. At the end of the day, we figured that if it all went to hell, we were young and we could move again. (This thought came before the car ride to Idaho actually happened. After our second cross-country trip, the only place we would be moving would be to the next block.) Also, we figured that the worst thing would be that we'd hate it, but in the interim, the boys would get to know one set of their grandparents better. And that wouldn't be bad at all.

Could we do it? Were we nuts? Unlike the proposed move before it, we had *zero* job prospects lined up. That is zero with a "z" in a town with roughly 1% of the available jobs of Austin. The added bonus was we were effectively torpedoing any career advancement—especially if my plan of opening a restaurant didn't come to pass—as well as our kids' educations. We knew four people in Sandpoint, two of them relatives and two were friends of relatives. So we knew four dinosaurs: not a soul within two decades of us. We knew shit about snow: snow shoveling, studded snow tires, or de-icer. (I now know that de-icer can ruin concrete and I have the driveway to prove it.)

Unlike many Hos we don't hunt or camp; in fact, we absolutely hate camping or anything that resembles it.

Our idea of a vacation is by no means sleeping on dirt, freezing our asses off, and starting a fire in order to cook, let alone shitting in the woods. Forget it. We knew nothing of the schools, neighborhoods, or the fact that winter lasted 14 months.

"But," I *didn't* say or *even think* at the time, "this would please both Mssrs. Frost and Campbell! It would be a road much less taken and I would again be following my bliss."

Decision made: Sandpoint, Idaho, here we come. Young and stupid equals brave.

THREE

....

UP AND TO THE LEFT

Before Kim's parents moved there, I had never heard of Sandpoint, Idaho. Like 90% of Americans, I could only name one place in Idaho: Boise. OK, maybe the Snake River Canyon, thanks to Evel Knievel and his rocket-powered "sky cycle." And, of course, I could only associate Idaho with one thing: yes, potatoes. Yet I could easily name a handful of ski towns, despite not strapping on ski boots until I was in my 30s. Likewise, I could name towns that were justly famous for water or for beautiful scenery. Hell, I could even name towns that were known simply because no one wanted to live there at all. Sandpoint, though, was a stealth town.

Sandpoint, Idaho is approximately a 45-minute drive from Canada to the north, and Montana to the east. This is actually how I explain to people where I am from. It gives a perspective: the panhandle's geography is actually a stark contrast to what many perceive Idaho to be: one giant potato patch. Town proper is situated on the shores of Lake Pend Oreille, a French phrase meaning "ear hanging" or "pendant." How the lake was named is disputed: was it named because the lake is shaped like an ear, or was it named for the Kalispel tribe that inhabited the area and favored that kind of look? It is an alpine lake fed from snowmelt via the Clark Fork and Pack Rivers. It is the largest lake in Idaho, and one of the deepest in the United States. It is so deep that during World War II, and to a small extent today, the US Navy conducted sonar testing there as it closely replicated ocean depths and characteristics. It is also damn cold. A few areas of the lake freeze over by January, encouraging intrepid ice fishers to drill their holes and stare into them. In the shallower areas, the ice is deep enough to allow for ice skating. The lake isn't warm enough to swim until June or so, but it rewards swimmers with pristine, clear blue water.

Once we ran off the Kalispel tribe and others—or rather, relocated them to land we didn't want—Sandpoint, served by the arrival of rail, became a rough-around-the-edges logging town. This is the Northwest after all, and we have scores upon scores of trees, mostly majestic evergreens that, viewed from the air, cover the area like a plush green blanket. We are surrounded by three mountain ranges: the Selkirks, the Bitteroots, and the Cabinets. While we are well north, it is not as cold as you might think—certainly not the numbing, bleak cold of the Midwest or the Dakotas. But we do get our fair share of snow, allowing the local ski mountain, Mt. Schweitzer, to open most years by Thanksgiving. From the summit, Schweitzer offers views of the lake, Canada, and Montana in the distance. In winter, the town assumes a snow-sports mountain town vibe with locals, many of whom moved here for that very reason, joining in with powder hounds visiting from other states.

Summers, with an average temperature of 81 degrees, are glorious. The vibe in summer shifts to a laid-back, almost beach town feel, with boats of all types dotting the lake. Due to its size, the brisk waters of Pend Oreille are rarely as crowded as the bath-water-warm Texas lakes I grew up around. Summers and winters are so beautiful, in fact, that many locals know to do any traveling in the spring, when the weather is a crapshoot and there's nothing to do outdoors. If you've got the cash, or don't care about having any cash, Sandpoint is a visually striking place to live.

To get there, at least from our home in Austin, the route indicated across non-sequential pages of the Rand McNally Atlas, that we needed to drive "up and to the left." First we had to sell the house. Even though the Austin economy was in the tank at the time, our house sold relatively quickly, thanks to one of those sales services that come in and make your house look nothing like it would if real people lived there. As usual, we were still packing boxes when the moving truck arrived.

Every time I move I am struck by how much worthless junkyard crap people hold on to, and even better, we actually move it from place to place with us. That "beauty" of a torchon lamp that we bought in the late 80s, with its white plastic shade and collapsible shaft, made four moves with us. Really. You come to the realization that your stuff is *actually junk* when it sits sadly on the lawn in the glaring sunlight, waiting to be put into the moving truck. You start engaging in banter and making excuses for your stuff to the movers, who couldn't care less why you bought this crap in the first place.

Me: "You know, bean bag chairs work wonders if you have a bad back. In fact, if I get in the right position, it is very similar to a zero-gravity chair that you see on Brookstone, but for a lot less."

Mover: "Hmmmph. How much more stuff you got?"

Me: "It's the place with all of those catalogues and now they're in airports—you should check them out."

Mover: *(walks away)*

In the case of our movers, all they cared about was trying to cram two hours of work into four.

For the move itself our plan was that I would drive the main truck, a big yellow underpowered Ryder rental, while Kim and the boys would follow in the Chevy Suburban, freshly outfitted with a portable DVD player that plugged into the cigarette lighter. This sounds so quaint now in the age of technology, but at the time it was pure magic. Behind the Ryder, we towed our Jeep Grand Cherokee on a sled or trailer-whatever-thing, taxing even more the truck's anemic power plant. If you have never driven a big truck, it can be dicey at times but after a while you get used to it. If you haven't driven one while towing a 3500-pound car behind it, I will tell you this: backing up is simply not an option. Also, you aren't supposed to drive faster than 45 miles per hour at any given time. I had zero confidence maneuvering this truck-trailer-rig in any direction other than a straight line. The one time I was forced to back up in some truck stop (in and of itself an anxiety-producing place) was one of the most nerve-racking moments of my life.

We were to drive across the country in four equal-spaced days, with three small boys under the age of six, on a limited budget. This was a dream come true. Unfortunately, the dream took a hit on the first day. It seems that mud flaps are required on the rear tires of a big truck, and ours was lacking those on the driver's side. We would have to wait for these to be procured and installed. We were assured that this wouldn't take long, so we decided to say *bon voyage* to our favorite McDonalds to kill some time and feed the kids in hopes of then buying a little extra time on the highway. It was early spring and unseasonably hot, even by Texas standards, so an air conditioned McDonalds wouldn't be all bad. The one we were saying goodbye to was very near our old house on Bee Caves Road, a new facility with an above average playscape that the kids loved. Our youngest, Sam, was wee, so we strapped him to a high chair at our table and let the other two boys, Austin the eldest, and Jackson the middle child, run amok in the fully-enclosed playscape.

"Ma'am, is that your son?" One of the part-time teenagers who was wiping down the adjacent table was looking at, and directing the question to, Kim. We had been occupied with Sam and talking about the move, so her question came as a bit of a surprise. "Um, the naked one at the top of the slide?" Jackson has long been the most heat-sensitive of our kids. He is the Goldilocks of temperature and humidity. It turned out that he had worked up a bit of a lather chasing his older brother, and there and then decided it was time to take off all of his clothes. He stood at the summit of the slide, about to make a bare-ass run, with a devil-may-care smile on his face. At least that was his plan until his mother launched herself out the door to inform him this restaurant had a dress code: clothes.

An ignominious start to the trip. Our first day dwindled waiting on those flaps, but we eventually got on the road. By the time we hit the highway it was rush hour, and we made it a grand total of 100 miles, stopping for the night in Waco. We could have pushed through into the night, as I once did from Houston to Tucson in one trip, subsisting on Diet Cokes and pork rinds. Kids, however, need proper nutrition and rest. Simple math will tell you that this didn't bode well for the other three days of driving.

We were traveling in early spring, so we were expecting some fairly large swings in weather: warm in Texas, but by the time we reached farther "up" it would likely be much cooler, with a chance of snow. We were just not prepared for the snow to fall in New Mexico.

Not just snow.

A blizzard.

That closed the road.

While we were on it.

We were happily driving on Interstate 40 leaving Texas and traveling into New Mexico, relieved to actually put some miles behind us, when it started to snow. This is not exactly the weather that snaps into your head when you think of New Mexico and Texas, but apparently it can happen. In that particular stretch of highway, there is nothing for miles. Wasteland. Nowhere to pull over. As the snow got to be particularly hairy, we heard on the radio that the highway was now closed due to inclement weather. Prior to that day, when I saw folks on television who had been stranded in snowstorms, I used to think, "Dumb bastards. Didn't they listen to the weather?" But on that day all I thought was, "Holy shit, I am driving an oversized Ryder truck with a car sled on the back." I also thought my wife and kids were in a two-wheel-drive Suburban. (Of course we bought a two-wheel drive. It was cheaper than a four by four, and we reasoned—absolutely incorrectly at the time—that we would never have a need for four-wheel-drive.)

And Kim and I *both* thought it was long past time to feed the *velociraptor.*

The raptor, cute in appearance to the uninitiated, was our one-year-old, Sam. He would ride in his car seat, happy as a clam waiting for the chance to see my big ole Ryder, and sing out, "Daddy Slop!" (Dad's truck!) But this little towhead was, and had always been, a vicious eating machine. We had nicknamed him the *velociraptor* since when we passed him one of those little zwieback crackers over the top of his reverse-facing car seat, all we would see was one of his little mitts reach out, snare it, and then promptly disappear from whence it came. At the time of our move, he was in the middle of a growth spurt and ate like a stevedore, with the diapers to prove it.

It started to dawn on us that it was time for Kim to nurse Sam about a half hour after we heard the announcement, but stopping was not an option. The conditions were near white-out, the shoulders of the highway a graveyard of jack-knifed eighteen-wheelers. The raptor was asleep, but he was a small, cute, ticking time-bomb. In the interest of self-preservation, I turned down the volume on my Radio Shack handheld that Kim and I were using to communicate: there was more than one storm coming. However, the ruts in the road created by the snow induced such a rocking motion inside the car that the little jackal didn't wake up for the entire three-hour stretch, effectively skipping a meal for the first time in his life.

I'm not sure how we made it through that whiteout, but I suspect the fear-induced slow and steady pace without stopping allowed both vehicles to maintain a delicate hold on the road that had not yet turned to ice. White-knuckled, we finally arrived in Albuquerque, where we booked an impossibly small room in a hotel that quickly sold out. That night we celebrated being alive with some stiff martinis and mediocre steaks at the local Outback restaurant.

That wasn't the last of the snow, but the second round wasn't trying to kill us—rather, it welcomed us to the West. We had just barely made it over the Continental Divide. On that particular stretch of highway, a relentless climb leaving Wyoming and entering Montana, I had my foot to the floor of the feeble Ryder, never moving the speedometer needle past 45mph. At one point, I was wondering whether I would just eventually roll to a shuddering stop. They say that the fear of public speaking is, for many people, more powerful than the fear of death. For me, scarier yet is an automotive malfunction in the middle of a busy highway. But on an uphill climb in the middle of nowhere? I just hoped "Daddy Slop!" could do what The Little Engine could.

Relief washed over me when we crested the hill and descended into Butte, Montana, greeted by big, puffy, late-season snowflakes. Butte, we now know, is the "butte" of jokes by Montanans. This might be due to the fact that the town has shrunk by almost two-thirds since its heyday as a mining town. It might be that all that used mine water has had a certain negative effect on its population and their offspring. It might just be because the town is ugly. It didn't matter to us: we had dodged snow and wind and crested the Rockies—admittedly not in heroic pioneer fashion, but for us it was an accomplishment. The snow flew, and we felt we'd made it; we were effectively one day removed from reaching Sandpoint, so a small celebration was in order. We found a Best Western with ample parking for our caravan and rented *two rooms,* not one. We bought Kentucky Fried Chicken and two bottles of wine. The adults got drunk while the kids, fueled by nothing more than scientifically enhanced chicken, treated their own room as if they were in a 70s rock band.

The next day we pushed through Montana into Idaho, and when we hit Coeur d'Alene we turned north: only 40 miles left in the journey. Our little circus was coming to town.

FOUR

....

THE NEW NORMAL

When you first drive past it, you do a double-take.

TERVAN.

That's what it says on the sign that juts out from the roof of a one-story building on the main drag in Sandpoint. You are puzzled, it looks like a . . . and it dawns on you: TAVERN. And for confirmation, the sign over the door itself reads: *The Tam O'Shanter*, in a jaunty font, with neon beer signs lighting the windows. For further confirmation, if you crane your neck around as you drive past on this one-way street, the other side of the sign gets it right: TAVERN. Of course, no one knows how long the sign has been this way: *it just is*. And no one calls the place, home to some of the coldest beer in town with an interior the size of a doctor's waiting room, its God-given name. It is the TERVAN. The beauty of this is that this misspelled sign is one of the first things you see when you arrive in Sandpoint. Every time I see this sign, it brings me joy.

The sign is located on a building in the downtown core. To get to that core, you must first drive across the Long Bridge, which is what we did years ago, beleaguered from our cross-country travels.

The Long Bridge is so named, I assume, because it is, well, long. It is instantaneously striking, motoring along I-95 through relatively nondescript country, exiting what seems to be a chute, to have a vista open up before you that is a sudden explosion of blues and greens. Lake Pend Oreille sparkles on either side of the 1.25-mile bridge providing the blues, with Roman Nose, part of the Selkirk Mountains, a beacon due north. The greens: an impossible amount of trees.

Of course, at the time we didn't pause to appreciate the jaw-dropping beauty. We drove our caravan straight to Kim's parents without delay. Our family of five was going to share their two-bedroom lakefront home with them for the next week until our apartment was ready. Their home, situated on Oden Bay, had commanding views of the lake, the town of Hope in the distance, and just beyond that, yes: Beyond Hope. Dropping off from their back deck was a three-tiered lawn and every type of flowering bush available at the local nursery.

I will say at the outset that I am fortunate that I like my in-laws. At least I did then, when they were younger and less old. It was not terribly uncomfortable squeezing into their house, and this still felt like an adventure. Kim and I shared the guest bedroom, living out of our suitcase. I don't know where the kids slept—somewhere, I think. Probably pretend camping, on the floor with some wadded up pillows and blankets. But they were happy, and our kids could sleep in an elevator shaft if they were tired enough. The living room was a riot of toys and highchairs and debris. My in-laws were clearly past this point in their lives, as I dreamt about being at some point, but they were glad to see Kim and the boys and so it was a grand little time.

We arrived on a weekend, and after a couple of detox days we planned on taking care of essential items, especially since we had no jobs to report to the next week. The first thing we did was rid ourselves of "Daddy Slop" and unhook the Jeep. We took it over to the muffler shop/repair shop/Ryder truck rental facility/notary public. At first this cafeteria of a business seemed amusing, but now it seems a necessary business survival mechanism for small towns. It's not hard to figure out, really. Other than when a big employer lays off a bunch of people and they run screaming back to California, there really is no big demand in our town for a Ryder truck dealership. But there is *some* demand. So a business in a similar industry like, say, a muffler shop with extra parking, might take on a truck rental franchise. In Sandpoint there are some multi-tasking businesses that require looking through a special pair of spectacles to figure out. There is the plant nursery/video rental store. This one probably evolved since the growing season here is about an hour long. But video rental? I suppose at the time this bolt of lightning struck the owners, videos were still being rented. Then there is the sub *shoppe*, inspiring that old world flair with the extra "e" in the name, that is also an antiques *shop*. The word "antiques" must have sufficient gravitas that an extra "e" is not required. Of course, the gas station has a teriyaki restaurant, and the local Radio Shack sells sheepskin slippers and blankets. Radio Shacks might have exited the earth years ago, but here we still believe.

Another thing we believe—at least a vocal, voting minority that can win elections does—is that a man's property is a man's property goddammit. The proof is that in 1997, our newly elected county commissioners abolished Sandpoint's building department and fired all the employees in one fell swoop. This meant that "Cooter" could be his very own contractor. And so we have quite a smorgasbord of housing styles and self-built remodels. These structures are not hard to find in our area. Just look for the house that has a somewhat normal footprint, and then takes a hard right with an add-on; or better yet, takes that hard right and then decides to shoot up a floor with the second story kind of riding piggyback, or kind of humping the first floor, depending on your outlook. If that house has the luxury of having the same color paint and siding, then it looks like an interesting but ugly mix of shapes and angles.

There are no Frank Gehrys in Northern Idaho.

Of course, we do have professionally built homes here: those that are manufactured and driven to their addresses, and those that are assembled on-site. Some of the latter are very old, like the house we ultimately wound up purchasing. Some homes are quite grand. These normally are lakefront or mountain properties, the ubiquitous, nouveau lodge dwellings replete with huge beams (extra points if they are whole logs; extra extra points if they are reclaimed wood). It's funny how you like something when you are not surrounded by it. When we lived in Texas I grew tired of, and eventually hated, limestone facades and brick. Now I kind of like it. In California, I loved all things Western and even read that dreadful magazine *Cowboys and Indians*, with its air-brushed covers of aging movie stars who are no more cowboys than, well, I am. I am certain that anyone would love being a cowboy if your cabin is 15,000 square feet, and you don't have to split wood for the log stove. Now that I live in the West, I am weary of log homes, log furniture, and absolutely anything decorative that is made with a chainsaw. I like logs in an active fireplace.

Another chore we decided to take care of right away, after returning the truck, was to get new Idaho drivers' licenses. It seemed idealistic, but we planned to take care of that chore, do some grocery shopping, grab some lunch, and find any parks in the area for the kids to run around. We were hoping to be home in time for happy hour because spending that much time with our kids while doing chores would make anyone drink.

We were done with all of it in two hours.

The California DMV helped trigger a move out of the state. The Bonner County Idaho DMV made me doubt reality. The motor vehicle offices are approximately the size of a corner store, with a total of two clerks. There are a few chairs, the requisite number of potted plants dotting the office, and country music playing softly on a boom box by the copier machine. There are no lines, no number system. There is—save the times of year when the latest drivers education class matriculates and must have their license *now*—no waiting. Savor that, city dwellers: almost immediate service. At a government agency. I think I might have giggled.

This lack of waiting in line happily persists in almost all services. Starbucks. Voting on election day. The Post Office. The P-o-s-t O-f-f-i-c-e. It's cute, yet insidious: this lack of waiting, lack of traffic, and lack of any mean-ingful driving distance more than a few miles, becomes the new normal. More than that, it becomes your right, so much so that the thought of driving to another city to shop at Wal-Mart becomes a deterrent. It doesn't matter that the other city is exactly six minutes away. And if there happens to be a line in Starbucks, which does hap-pen in the summer months as the town population swells by a factor of three, someone like me becomes unhinged. It didn't take too long for one thing to be-come abundantly clear: what you might lose in culture, choices, convenience, innovation, income, and diversity, you more than make up for in time saved.

The exception to this fantastic new superpower of being unfettered by waiting might be grocery shopping. There are two reasons for this. First, everybody knows everybody, so the chances are quite good that you will run into someone you know which will require time-killing conversation. Like a high school reunion, it can be a minefield of people you would otherwise avoid. And you can always accurately predict who you will see according to the grocery store they frequent. Safeway: Jack, Diane, Geraldine. Yokes: Annie, Monica, Carol, Lisa. Super 1 Foods: Stefanie, Phyllis, Sydney, Marty.

The second reason might be zig-zagging aisles to avoid service providers you have abandoned. It is the tyranny of a small town: fear of breaking up with your doctor, dentist, or hair stylist. Quite a few friends still see health care professionals they do not like – at all – but remain under their care, afraid to leave. Of course, this doesn't just happen in the grocery store where you might play a cat-and-mouse game, or busy yourself studying the ingredients list on a can of peanut butter. Soccer fields are a prime example of when we have changed course and tacked around entire fields to dodge a doctor or dentist we've fired. In a city, you would simply switch to a new health care professional. You would most likely request that your new doctor or dentist obtain your records from your old provider. Easy. You would never see them again. Not so in a small town. Having been through a number of dentists and doctors before finding one I was comfortable with, I came up with a pricey yet spineless solution: start fresh. I had each new provider treat me like a newborn, ordering up new X-rays and anything else necessary.

I was not alive when JFK was assassinated, but like every American alive on 9/11, I can tell you exactly where I was and what I was doing that dark day (burning "sins" off of a watch). I can also tell you exactly where I was when I *suggested* to my wife that her hair, uh, looked wonky. We were standing in the kitchen of our rental apartment about six months after we moved in. I thought I handled the issue like a zookeeper who knows that yes, tigers have teeth. I skirted the issue well, and *suggested* that she might consider looking into a different style or cutter, that her hair didn't suit her:

"I won't be home until six on Thursday. I have a hair-cut."

"Are you still seeing the same stylist?"

"Yes. Why?"

"I think I hear the boys calling me. Be right back."

"Wait. Why did you ask if I'm still going to the same stylist? Does it look like I switched?"

"I thought you said you were going to try someone else. That you weren't happy with your hair."

"I never said that. Why would I say that?"

"Maybe I just dreamt it. I have really wild dreams when I eat too much—like last night. One too many ta-cos. I think I even saw a story about that on the news last week..."

"Do you think I should switch stylists? Do you not like my hair?"

BEHOLD: THE ABYSS.

"Well, I'm not sure it flatters your face."

I used to think that in the tricky subject department, weight vs. hair, that weight would win hands down. Now, I am not so sure. Suffice to say the look she gave me was not one of tenderness. However, she did find a new stylist who was booked a solid four months out. As are all the local hair stylists who are not ham-handed, self-taught, or Wal-Mart or Supercuts employees.

For a male of the species, where to get a haircut is not necessarily that difficult or important, at least not for me. At the time, my luxurious mane was thinning to the point of having to make a Rudy Giuliani or Matt Lauer decision, so it really didn't pose too big a problem. Any trade school intern could have cut my hair; all I wanted was a barbershop where I could shoot the breeze while looking at *Sports Illustrated* or possibly, just possibly, a *Playboy* magazine tucked safely away in an opaque binder.

On a lark, I chose a barbershop just outside the town core that was wedged between a pet store and a store specializing in engraving. The pet store is the reason I found the barbershop. I had gone in a few weeks prior, entertaining the idea of getting the kids some goldfish or maybe a turtle. As I browsed the aisles, debating how long a goldfish or turtle would survive the care of three boys under the age of six, an early 70s Oldsmobile wagon careened into the lot. The kind with the tailgate that went both up *and* down with the turn of a key. It was not driven by a customer: it was the rat lady. This entrepreneur brought in a cardboard box teeming with rats, to sell to the pet store. I had never seen anything like this, although I suppose pet store rats have to come from somewhere. They were crawling all over each other as she plopped them into the glass aquarium where they no doubt would await their untimely end, purchased by a snake owner. I'm not sure if seeing dozens of teeming rats influenced my decision, but I decided to pass on pets just then.

The barbershop itself had the ubiquitous barber pole out front. It also had multiple signs espousing positions on local politics that I did not yet understand. I did not see, however, that it also sported a Confederate flag. Yessiree. The Stars and Bars.

Of course, the area surrounding our town has had a bad reputation for harboring white supremacists—why, Ruby Ridge occurred not 45 minutes outside our town. I even know some people who are preparing for the Great War or the Great Famine, or when the government decides to turn on us and brother kills brother, or some other hocus-pocus. But these racists are for the most part long gone, or at least not operating in plain sight. So, in I went. Toto, we're not in Kansas anymore. We've gone through the looking glass. I believe those are mixed references and for that I apologize, but you get the drift.

First clue: no *Playboys*, no sports magazines. Only *Soldier of Fortune* and *Reloader* magazines. Second clue: the kind of scary looking guy who was to cut my hair sported shooting glasses, a clear green accountant's visor like you might see in an old western, and a garter on his arm. He was short and stocky with jet black hair. I sat in the chair and immediately my hair care professional asked me where I was from. Hmmm. Where to pick? California, where my wife and I had lived for the past dozen years or so? Or Texas where I hailed from, and from where we had recently moved? The self-preservation part of me decided on Texas.

"I'm from Texas."

My barber, we'll call him Mr. GunsAndAmmo, gave an approving grunt and followed with, "At least you're not from California, those people are ruining this area." Yes indeed.

"Them damn people come here and act like they own the place. Try and change things. Well I tell you what. Things have been just fine here without 'em. They should all go back where they came from."

"It's nice and warm out today. I sure don't miss the Texas heat!"

"Tell you another thing. They're driving up our property taxes. Not to mention, a lot of them are anti-gun and anti-hunting. Bet they haven't read the Second Amendment to our United States Constitution. 'The right of the people to keep and bear Arms shall not be infringed.' You hunt?"

"Well, no. I've been bird hunting before, and I like it, just not a deer hunter or any animals like that."

"Well, sir, you are missing out. There is nothing tastier in this world than fresh elk liver, cooked up with onions and bacon and gravy. Got to be fresh, mind you."

After 10 minutes or so of me listening and him talking, I decided to ask Mr. GunsAndAmmo about his trade. Plus, I was curious. I remember as a kid seeing my dad fully reclined in the barber chair, his face swaddled in steaming towels. After 10 minutes or so, Hector, our mutual barber, had to wake Dad up so he could shave his softened beard with a freshly stropped straight razor.

"Do you all give shaves anymore?"

Mr. GunsandAmmo, with satisfaction replied, "Nope. The *queers* ruined it for everyone. All their AIDS blood."

Those words actually came out of his mouth.

FIVE

....

THE WEDNESDAY BREAK-
FAST CLUB

Mrs. Magoo caught a girder before I did. I think it took Kim all of two weeks to land a new job in a new town in an industry in which she had never worked. She is smart, I'll give her that. She is attractive, I'll give her that too. But this was ridiculous. Fantastic—yet ridiculous. She simply shopped her resume around town to some local Certified Public Accountants wondering if they needed any help, or knew of any job possibilities. One of them had worked with a local bank vice-president in another life in Alaska. He interviewed her and just happened to be one of the few bankers who would consider hiring someone with no industry experience for that level position. The banking industry, I know now, is very fraternal in its hiring policies.

"Mrs. Magoo, we need a controller, when can you start?"

Before we moved, I decided to get back into the restaurant business. I have that disease that most in the industry have and it is hard to shake. Plus, I thought I was relatively good at it. We had decided that the end goal was to open our own restaurant, but in the meantime I would take anything to make a living. So, ultimately a new restaurant would be the girder I was hoping to grab, but for now, I was open to anything. That was not as easy as it sounded, and I was still looking.

Not long after Kim landed her new job, we became fast friends with her new boss. We had dinner with him two to three times a week, as he was recently divorced. He introduced us to multiple people, and though we didn't realize it at the time, we eventually would buy his house when a new job took him out of town. One of the people he introduced us to when I was visiting Kim at work one day was one of his better customers, an owner of a construction company that also had moved from California. This guy was a talker, gregarious as hell, who had come to Idaho for the freedoms that California lacked. He told us that day, his feet kicked up on our banker friend's desk, that he and a group of guys met every Wednesday morning for breakfast and why don't I come along? Since one of the other guys was also a friend, and I needed to meet people—despite the associated pain of meeting people—I decided to give it a go. Also, my calendar was blank, apart from dropping off resumes and looking at online job boards, and the kids were happily ensconced for the morning and early afternoon in a terrific daycare that we had just found.

We met for breakfast at a nice, but sadly empty, coffee shop and lunch place. The other members in the Wednesday Morning Breakfast Club included a soccer coach, a bricklayer, a friend who owned a sporting goods shop, and our founding father: construction guy. While we all had relocated to Sandpoint, I was the new kid on the block; they had all lived in Sandpoint for at least three years at that point. They knew more people than I did. They also knew the ropes, the rumors, and in some cases, the truth.

Scales fell from my eyes when I heard the story about a local professional who liked to cavort naked in his backyard with a local barista. Or the guy who was trapped naked in the closet of his cuckolding mistress. I discovered numerous cases of breastular enhancement. I learned of a gentleman whose parked car literally slid sideways down the side of the ski mountain while he was visiting a friend's wife. The backstories to the cover stories Kim and I had been told reminded me of three card monte: even with your eyes open, even if you're attuned, things aren't always as they appear.

They warned me not to have lunch with anyone except my wife, lest I be talked about as an adulterer. When dining with a female, the safe, acceptable size of the party was three. I was informed of the politics of our youth soccer league. In Sandpoint, "the beautiful game" had skeletons in its closet. And if I was the member of a church, I was warned not to drink excessively in public, or often. Thankfully, I am an occasional Catholic. We consider that a prerequisite: excessively often.

After breakfast, construction guy invited us to his house to shoot some skeet. I happen to really enjoy shotgun sports, despite the fact that I'm not really a hunter. I enjoy the craftsmanship of the guns, and the sport, so I said yes. With no job and the kids in day care, what the hell else was I going to do?

When we arrived at construction guy's house, I realized that we had to take four-wheelers and dirt bikes up to the shooting area. We gathered in the garage and picked out our guns. This was not hard since there were about 60 or so lying around. It was a smorgasbord of firepower. I wondered why they weren't locked up, with his kids running around. I was assured, however, that there was no need to lock up guns when children (and adults) have been taught how to properly use and treat firearms. I could not disagree more with that particular sentiment, yet years later, I am struck by the disparate viewpoints on gun control, gun ownership and hunting that exists between city dwellers and rural communities. And how, depending on where you live, both viewpoints make perfect sense.

I had never driven a four-wheeler, but I was game and looked around for a helmet. No helmets. OK, I thought, not exactly like California, where helmet use is a law, but this is Idaho. Welcome! Pretty soon we were screaming along trails with rocky drop-offs not six feet from the wheels. I was on the back of one of the dirt bikes holding on uncomfortably to a man I had met only hours before. I had supreme confidence in his driving ability that I knew nothing about.

When we arrived at the actual shooting area, on land owned by someone *other* than my new friend, it was nothing more than a series of uneven, angled, rocky slabs overlooking a valley below. We were going to balance on the slanted rocks, with live ammunition, while one of us launched a clay pigeon into the air using a manual slinger. This made perfect sense. As we readied to shoot, I looked around for hearing protection. No hearing protection. I had never shot without hearing protection, but thought, well, these guys must do it all the time. After blasting away for half an hour, I had the eardrums of Pete Townshend. During a break in shooting, one of my fellow breakfast club members suggested that we push some rocks off the cliff. Now this was some good old-fashioned hillbilly fun! Forget the question I wanted to ask but did not: why? What I *did* ask was what might be below us that we were dumping these 500-pound rocks onto. All I got for my questions were sideways "what a pussy" glances, and no answer that made any sense. Not that the whole exercise made a micron of sense, anyway. I decided to refrain from this little sport, thinking the whole time that if there were hikers down there, they (and we!) were in serious trouble. Death from above.

But happily, the fun wasn't over yet. Construction guy proposed that we take the four-wheelers to the top of one of the local mountains, Mount Baldy. Our merry band thought this was a capital idea. Since we had only two four-wheelers and five guys, some of us had to ride on the backs. These particular four-wheelers had no back seats. They were equipped for only the pilot, and the very likely tattooed, overweight co-pilot. They did, however, have a small bed in back, on which I imagine you are supposed to strap your fresh kill. It was a lot like riding on a very hard wooden surface while hitting rocks and potholes. No it was not like that—it was exactly that. Riding on a hard wooden surface with metal side rails to keep you on board, while hitting rocks and potholes. I was just happy that I had eaten a nice big breakfast.

About three-quarters of the way up the mountain we hit snow, since this was May and the snow had not yet melted. We were in what we call around here, "the mud season." It's just what it sounds like: soft mud from spring rains and melting snow, swollen rivers and creeks, and in the case of Mount Baldy, snowpack. In fact, there is a local wives' tale that is more often than not true: don't plant your summer garden until Baldy melts. This snowpack eventually stopped us dead in our tracks.

What are five dipshits to do?

"Uh, I guess that's it, huh? We have to turn around?"

"Nah, let's summit this bitch!"

"Yeah!"

"Yeah!"

"Yeah!"

"Aw shit, OK."

Sir Edmund Hillary then proposed we get out and push the heavy four-wheelers up the slushy mountainside, all the way to the top, while wearing improper footwear. For no sane reason. And that's just what we did. We disembarked, landed in knee-deep snow, and began pushing these heavy-ass things uphill. The entire time I was questioning their sanity and my own, and it felt like one of those bad movies where the nice guy gets involved with a bunch of thugs, and lo and behold they rob a bank on a dare or kill somebody. I was that guy. And these guys weren't thugs, they just appeared to have a more fully refined sense of fun than my own. Thankfully close to the top, we were all out of breath, and consensus said we were close enough: abandon ship. Thank you Jesus.

So, back down the mountain we went to grab the three dirt bikes we had left at the shooting range. Even though I had no helmet, was driving close to the edge of a ravine, and was making only my second trip on a four-wheeler, I pegged the throttle at the maximum, relieved to get off that hill in one piece and not as a criminal. And, I have to admit, grinning all the while, because if you check your logic and fear at the door, these four-wheelers are a gas. But the fun with this group didn't stop then. We were going to Elk Camp together.

If it's October in Sandpoint, you can pretty much write off having your toilet fixed, your roof shingled, or your furnace checked, because October, my friends, is the beginning of elk season, and most in the trades are out hunting. Entire families hunt—men, women, and children. Locals and hunters call it "elk fever." They proudly display "elk fever" stickers in the rear windows of their pickup trucks, along with silhouettes of elk and deer, and in some cases, their artillery of choice.

For anyone who has the fever, elk season is a huge deal. And since the elk don't come to you and wait patiently to be shot, dressed, and packaged, you have to go to them. It turns out those bastards live high up in mountainous terrain, far from town. Also, it seems that to shoot them you have to, in many cases, hike that terrain for what could be miles. If you are lucky enough to bag one, that means dealing with that terrain again, only this time hauling hundreds of pounds of elk carcass. And it also seems that since it is October in Northern Idaho, it will likely be as cold as a well digger's ass. Because of all of these factors, and I guess because some people actually seem to like camping, they set up elk camps.

The locations of some of these are deathbed secrets. Construction guy had his own elk camp in the rugged terrain near the town of Clark Fork, close to the Montana border, and I was flattered when he invited me to

visit camp for a few days. I was flattered, but didn't realize that this was probably a tax write-off for him since
his contracting company was slated to eventually build
our restaurant.

I was pretty excited, since up to this point I had been
regaled with stories of how fantastic this camp was. Multiple heated tents, with carpeting no less. A mess tent
with a three-meals-a-day menu posted on a white board,
all cooked by construction guy's wife. I did not hunt elk
(but have no problem with it and love to eat it) but I was
game for at least one night of drinking, bullshitting and
cigar smoking. So I figured what the hell.

When I drove into the mountains it was a grey day
pissing rain—not all that unusual for Northern Idaho at
that time of year. Apparently, one of the endearing
things about elk hunting is that the weather is the abso-
lute shits when you hunt. You earn your trophy. I followed the directions to the camp, but of course got lost.
In my defense, I was traveling on old logging roads. This
means no street signs, no lampposts. Those old National
Forest roads go on for miles in different directions. One
wrong turn and you could be lost for days. It really is
chilling if you think about it, and I thought about it
plenty.

Finally, when I was doubling back from a wrong turn,
I saw another unfortunate soul who also was invited to
the elk camp and I tailed him in. Camp appeared to be
empty, for the most part. Construction guy and his wife
were there, but everyone else was out on the hunt. They

gave me a tour with pregnant smiles on their faces: was this place grand or what? The tents were a series of ragged army surplus tents. Yes, there was an outhouse with a toilet. But that outhouse looked like the Lighthouse for the Blind put it together: it was a series of particleboards nailed together at odd angles. The toilet amounted to a toilet seat set over a hole in the ground. The carpeting in the tents was mud-streaked and damp, which helped enormously in making the tents moist and steamy when the portable heaters were on. The mess hall was actually the only thing that presented itself as I had imagined: another surplus tent, propane cookers, plenty of canned goods for the "freshly prepared" meals, and a dry erase board with the day's specials written on it.

As I was milling around, my fellow campers started straggling back from their miles of hiking to find their prey. No one had seen anything. This was not entirely surprising: elk, or *wapiti,* are known as the ghosts of the forest, incredibly elusive with the ability to disappear in thick stands of trees, and because of their coloring, virtually disappear while only feet away. It was about 4:00 in the afternoon, there was a constant drizzle blown sideways by the wind, and it was getting colder as it was getting dark. No beers were being broken out, the fire of now-wet fuel was smoking up the entire camp, and construction guy's compatriots were starting on an early dinner of canned pork and beans.

It took me less than one minute to decide I was not staying.

I had envisioned whisky and beer and cigars. If there is any redeeming thing at all about camping—there is not—it is drinking by the campfire. I told construction guy and the boys that I was leaving, with the flimsy excuse that I had just wanted to see what the camp was all about and had never intended to stay the night. In typical male fashion they jeered me. Peer pressure never ends. This was a bit different though. If they were offering a joint, that would be something else entirely. But jeering me into staying in a wet, cold, dirty camp with a bunch of guys I barely knew smoking 10 cent cigars?

I slept nice and cozy in my own bed that night.

SIX

....

LUNCH LADIES

Before I got the job, I interviewed with Farrah Fawcett-Majors.

No, of course not. Not the real Farrah Fawcett-Majors, just her doppelgänger. I was interviewing for the position of Kitchen Manager at the Snowpeak Mountain School (SMS.) Farrah, it turns out, was the outgoing kitchen manager. She was not leaving, but rather abdicating her throne after only two years on the job. The pressure (or as I would find out later, the bitches) had gotten to be too much. And to clarify, she only mirrored Farrah in the hair: it was regal.

Kitchen Manager at SMS was going to be my first job in Sandpoint! Not only was it a job, but it was an honest-to-goodness, career-paying job in the hospitality industry in Sandpoint. If there was a rarity scale, this would edge just ahead of the Loch Ness monster. Actually, it was not in Sandpoint, but was located about 35 miles north, near the village of Naples, Idaho. This Naples bears precious little resemblance to Naples, Italy. This Naples bears a better resemblance to a trading post, with its solitary gas station/general store, one-room school, and post office. It is rugged country located just south of Bonners Ferry, Idaho (cue banjo music) and perilously close to that famous landmark, Ruby Ridge, where Randy Weaver and his family were besieged by US Marshals and the FBI. The country around Naples is a breathtaking combination of two mountain ranges, the Selkirk Mountains to the west and the Cabinets to the east, framing a picturesque valley where the Kootenai River meanders on its way to British Columbia. Snow Creek Falls and Grouse Creek Falls, two of the myriad waterfalls in the area, are so beautiful that you would swear they were designed and built by Disney.

A downside to the job was going to be the commute. But despite bemoaning commutes and stating them as a reason for moving out of the crowded city, I now coveted a commute, any commute, that would help us keep the lights on. The drive to SMS takes about 45 minutes on Interstate 95, toward the Canadian border. The journey takes you past the Pack River, a shallow river that many people inner tube at different stretches; four hours of tranquility interrupted only by smacking mosquitoes. If I haven't already, I like to make the odd Deliverance joke about different parts of North Idaho, to give you the proper feel. But seriously, the Pack River area has it. If you were to turn off of I-95 in the Pack River area, you'd half expect to see Ned Beatty, with his pants around his ankles, or maybe have an arrow notched by Burt Reynolds whistle past your ear. More accurately: the Pack River types look nothing like the moonshine-swilling Southerners in Deliverance. Actually they look more like the alligator-eating, sister-dating coon asses from the movie Southern Comfort. The devil, they say, is in the details.

The school itself is located about 15 miles from the Naples exit, announced by a simple sign with the name of the school and an arrow pointing at a 45-degree angle: up and to the left. It is situated on a ridge just adjacent to Ruby Ridge. The road is dicey, with not much room for car or trucks passing from the opposite direction, and even less so in the winter with a decent snow fall. The road makes a sharp bend and then gathers altitude at a sharp angle. At this point the Kootenai River Valley is exposed, with huge firs on the side of the road framing the view. Once you arrive at the end of the road, the vista opens up to a giant clearing occupied by some basketball courts, and an impressive large mountain structure with some outlying buildings. It was beautiful yet isolated.

It is isolated and rugged for a reason.

SMS and other schools of its type are located way the hell out in the wilderness because they occupy a category called "behavioral wilderness programs" or "youth wilderness therapy programs." The translation is that these programs are for problem kids who need to be parked well away from the population to "get them back to nature" and "take them away from the temptations of the city" (explanations and rationalizations mine.) But more likely, and equally useful, they are located in East-Jesus to prevent the unlikely, yet very possible, escape. Snowpeak itself had two sister schools: Tamarack, located near Moyie Springs, Montana, and Treetop, which was just down the ridge from SMS. Treetop, I would find out later, would also be within my purview.

My interview with Farrah and her time-vacuum hair was a success, despite the fact that in my eagerness to land the job and my delight in meeting some new people, I violated just about every HR rule in the book. I offered up all sorts of things about myself that had nothing to do with the job, and even asked the cute HR director (benignly) if she was married. Just making conversation. Later that day, after driving back to Sandpoint, they called and offered me the job. Unwittingly, I was going down the rabbit hole—which largely ended up being an enjoyable one, but a rabbit hole nonetheless. Thankfully I was starting the job in the summer, so I was able to get used to the drive and facility before winter made things interesting.

Like the first day of any job I've had, the night before I woke up every hour on the hour nervous, largely about meeting new people and having a new routine. Misjudging the length of the drive and the complete lack of any sort of traffic, I got to work quite early. I didn't have a full campus tour, but rather started working with Farrah

Fawcett-Majors and shadowing her for the week before she handed over the keys. She seemed nice and quite capable, and mainly bitched about the staff and how lazy they were and how she couldn't deal with the pressure. Pressure? In a school cafeteria? One full of kids who had no choice where they could eat for miles all around? It turns out the pressure came from the fact that despite the extortionist tuition and fees, the school allowed only about $1.20 per kid per meal. This adds up to three meals for $3.60. Less than, in every ballpark in every city in the United States, a soda. (Clarification: yes I know, I know: much of the fee at a school like this goes to around-the-clock security, chaperones, nurses, clinicians, teachers, etc. But still, $1.20 per meal is ridiculous.)

I inherited a crew of what I imagine is every adult's memory of school cafeteria employees: lunch ladies. The average age of my lunch ladies was 60, give or take a decade, with three of them really throwing off the curve. There was Lacy, mid-30s or so with tattoos and long blonde hair, who had a daughter, lived in a trailer park and could drink like a longshoreman. She had a great personality and such a manic, contagious laugh, I often wondered if she was still drunk from the night before. Ethel was well north of 60, school marm-ish, supported her million year-old dad, was rigid in the way things were done, impatient with my youth and ideas (discovered later), and had a fondness for sitting down on the job. Literally. She sat on her very own stool cooking lunch. Sitting down on the job in a kitchen is, how do I say it? A killing offense. Betty was in her mid-70s and full of spunk and opinions. She was our afternoon cook, and Ethel's arch-nemesis. None of these women had any kitchen training except for Farrah, who had owned her own small restaurant and could really hump it when she had to—especially if working extra hard facilitated her role as martyr-in-chief. A lot of my time that year was spent mediating among these felines, and on more than one occasion having to resort to human resources to smooth things out. Seriously, those bitches sometimes acted like six-year-olds.

Each of the ladies had her own area of expertise. Betty, our night cook, was designated with making some casserole-y type thing and setting out the evening salad bar. Ethel, it turned out, was the lead cook for lunch, and since that was where I hoped to make the most improvement, was destined to be the pebble in my shoe with her standoffish, sour attitude. Lacy also worked nights and helped during the day. Bless her heart, she lacked a specialty, and really, the ability to cook. The meals I assigned her had to have kindergarten-level difficulty. And then there was Farrah. The self-proclaimed queen of the salad bar, she also set up breakfast due to her seniority and therefore early shift, and was the baker. Her cinnamon rolls, a source of great pride, were so sweet and frosted so thick with icing they could kill a diabetic.

There were, however, two pretty interesting aspects of the baking side of things. First, the chocolate chip cookies Farrah baked and then froze were preyed upon by the staff. Those little goodies were only made for the box lunches we sent out with the kids who had to go into town for work-study, or a doctor's visit. Normally when I think of box lunches, I think of classy ones like the cold roast chicken that Grace Kelly and Cary Grant enjoyed in To Catch a Thief. These were not those box lunches. These were about as polar opposite as you could get. These were pieces of aging white bread filled with three pieces of off-color luncheon meat and a sad piece of cheese. For good measure we gave them some comically inadequate single-serve mayonnaise and mustard packets, which we all knew couldn't dress the sandwich of a Keebler elf. That, some chips, and the cookie. The kids, maniacs maybe and depressed for certain, were of sound enough mind to take the chips and cookie and trash the rest. But these chocolate chip morsels were in such unfathomable demand that the staff would try to sneak into the kitchen to grab one. They would tiptoe past my office and slip into the walk-in freezer to get the loot. When I found out how much these things were in demand, I used them like an inmate uses cigarettes: as currency. Most often I used them to get things like computer fixes from the IT guy. Funny thing is, they were no better than Chips Ahoy, and yet those poor bastards were hooked on them—possibly because they lived and worked under the same dietary restrictions as the kids.

The second thing that was peculiar about baking was that we had to lock up the yeast for bread. Now, when I first arrived at the school, Farrah informed me that we locked up all knives and I could understand that, although it did feel a little like I was working in "the joint." But yeast? What were the kids going to do, run down the halls spraying yeast to and fro?

No. They would brew stuff. Now that, I thought to myself, was pretty fucking cool, not to mention industrious as hell.

The job itself was a basic food service manager's job with the usual requirements: menu planning, ordering, cooking, staffing, and profit and loss statement responsibility. Staffing, easily the biggest pain in the ass in food service, was thankfully a bit of a joke. We were open for three meals a day, yes. But breakfast consisted of yogurt, toast, juice, and monochrome canned fruit salad, laid out by one person. Lunch was the main meal with an abundant staff, and dinner usually amounted to some one-dish monstrosity that could be handled by one person. That person was out the door by 7pm or so, since the kids cleaned the kitchen. Saturday was "sugar cereal day." It was the only day the inmates were allowed to eat sugar cereal, and it was a feeding frenzy, in part because they were kids, and in part because they ate a ton of it to give themselves the only buzz available to them on the inside. I would have hated to be the school staff on those days. Those kids must have been pinballs. Sunday was brunch, another travesty of cooking that in no way resembled the type of meal that you drink your way through on Mother's Day. It was a smorgasbord of pre-cooked bacon, frozen waffles, and frozen crepes with ricotta cheese. The Ritz-Carlton it was not.

Since most of the old biddies were lifers, and since the unemployment rate in Naples was even higher than in Sandpoint, I was fully staffed except for a few random hours which Lacy covered, though the occasional bender precluded her from showing up.

During my first week at SMS I didn't have to plan any meals, which afforded me the time and opportunity to see what the kids were used to eating, and what products were on hand. A quick tour of the storeroom spoke sad volumes. We used so many canned goods that we had specially designed racks to deliver them to our waiting hands with speed and accuracy. I remember perusing some of these treats, many of which were used on the "fresh" salad bar. These were the salad bar version of greatest hits: beets and garbanzo beans and miniature corn. Things that have no other use than filling out a middling salad bar. And then there was the canned cheese sauce. Believe it or not, canned cheese has different strata of quality. There are the name brand types like Que Bueno! that should really only have a one-line descriptor: edible! But we carried a no-name brand whose descriptor might be: yellow! I wouldn't feed that shit to my cat. Or dog. I guess they fed it to the kids for their nacho bar or some such.

The first day I worked, Ethel proudly told me that she was making one of the kids' and staff's fav-O-rite meals: the ubiquitous Caesar salad with chicken. It was not what I was expecting to be served to a bunch of kids in the wilds of the Idaho Panhandle. At the same time, I was encouraged that maybe the stuff I found in the storeroom was the exception and not the rule. Well made, I love Caesar with chicken. Like most recipes with only a few ingredients, each one should be really good to make the dish shine. For this particular dish, you might be inclined to use a rotisserie chicken, or maybe a piece of grilled chicken breast. I would not recommend, however, using pre-cubed chicken meat out of pouch that itself came out of a 10-pound box. Using chicken that probably spent more time inside a machine than it did clucking around a barnyard does not necessarily spell doom, since the real game changer with a Caesar salad is the dressing. It's actually quite easy to make, blending lots of garlic with anchovies, eggs, lemon juice and olive oil. What did we make for the kids? We made the dressing by opening premium gallon jugs. We then tossed it with the chicken. But, I was assured by Ethel with a twinkle in her eye, there was a trick that made this version special. And that trick was to heat up the dressing in a pot on the stove prior to adding it to the chicken and ladling the whole hot mess over the previously cut, already bagged romaine lettuce. She was right. I hadn't seen that trick and it was indeed special.

That same week of training, or indoctrination, I was taken on a tour of Snowpeak's sister school that I was also responsible for, Treetop. Treetop was the maximum security felon-filled companion institution to SMS's minimum security white-collar-crime-filled country club. To get into Treetop, you had to have some pretty serious issues, and for the most part you don't enroll willingly. They come to you and get your ass. I met some of the guys who were the "getters" and they took kids against their will, but not their parents' wills. Parents were often complicit in schemes to allow the "getters" to practice their craft. One particular story involved parents duping their child into going out for a birthday dinner—the only way they could get him out of the house. Once in the car, the guys in white coats, or rather the guys in precision mountain gear, showed up. Often they came at night, seized the at-risk teenager, got on a plane with them, and off they went.

Once at Treetop, the kids were given wilderness clothing and moved into a compound in the woods, with very few creature comforts. The interesting thing about Treetop was that a lot of it—and I'm not sure it worked—was consequence driven; I suppose this was to teach the effects of one's actions and decisions. If you are cold, and we are cold in North Idaho a lot, why, you cut wood for the fire. Those kids cut a shitload of wood. Year-round, they walked across the property to SMS to pick up their communal meals. They walked over carrying food service warming boxes that were suspended between two wood poles like some sort of travois. When they arrived at SMS, they were not allowed to engage, speak to, or look at the kitchen staff. They had to turn their backs to us because they had not earned that right.

That's some creepy shit isn't it? I guess they were tough cases and needed to be torn down in order to be brought back up. My job, other than to feed them, was to make sure their own kitchens were stocked with canned goods for the meals that they made there.

When I say we fed them, it is impossible to overstate how much these urchins ate. They ate like wolves, probably from all that woodcutting. One of the items on the kitchen inventory that we supplied them—and this was also a bit puzzling, like the yeast—was prune juice. Yes, I know why: to keep them regular. But why? Well, it seems the prune juice was needed primarily during winter, when the little darlings would constipate themselves rather than have to walk to the outdoor shitters in the freezing cold.

Again, I say, industrious as hell.

Once they were no longer a threat to themselves or to the general population, they moved the half-mile to SMS. As part of their graduation, they had to complete a "ropes course" with their parents. One of the exercises in the course was to have either party belay the other while they were climbing. I suppose this New Age crap works, but I, for one, would sooner walk across the 405 freeway in LA than allow one of those little buggers to support me on a ropes course—especially if I had a hand in sending their ass there in the first place.

On the whole, Treetop creeped me out, so I steered clear of that place other than doing the occasional canned food inventory.

Once my week of training camp was over, it was time to step up and do some meal planning myself. I honestly cannot remember all of the meals that I planned over the course of the next year, but I do remember the very first meal. It wasn't anything fancy—far from it. It was supposed to be chicken in a fajita marinade, but I seriously bungled the amounts in the marinade so I made a quick spice rub to dry rub the chickens and then we were simply going to roast them. The trick, and the source of a near gran mal seizure on Ethel's part, was that to keep the costs low, I ordered whole chickens that had to be broken down into pieces the day before. The fact that they arrived partially frozen helped not one bit. Her expression, when I described her job that afternoon, was a mixture of intense constipation, schoolmarm anger, and a child's face right before he digs in his heels and throws a bitch of a tantrum. She muttered something like "it's impossible," to which I employed my favorite managerial response: "Of course you can, but once you get started, if you need help I'd be glad to jump in," along with a carpetbagger's smile.

With numb fingers, it took all four of us a couple of hours to get the job done. My fingers were frozen, fresh blisters from a knife raised on my hands. But there was no way on God's green earth I would say anything negative. I had to win this battle of wills. I don't remember the rest of the meal, rice and beans and guacamole I think, but I do remember two results. The entire staff and student body gave me a standing ovation—awkward as hell when you think, "I am not Madame Curie, I just baked some chicken." The second result? Boy genius had forgotten to line the sheet pans with pan liners or foil, so the spice rub bonded metallurgically with the pans, making them a dishwasher's nightmare. After the lunch meal, our staff did most of the dishes so they were doubly thrilled.

As many successful meals as we served, thanks to most of the staff embracing the change, there were many close calls and near-debacles. Most of these came when the combination of my ignorance of replicating certain recipes for large groups dovetailed with staggeringly poor cooking knowledge on our staff's part. Fettuccine Alfredo for 100? Actually fairly easy, albeit maybe not completely authentic, if you have the right equipment. Not impossible, though. But it got pretty dicey when Lacy dumped 20 pounds of fettuccine in a quantity of water suited for about five pounds of pasta. What happens then? Well, if you haven't stirred it adequately, and Lacy most certainly had not, the fettuccine fuses together, softening on the outside while keeping a crunchy core. Delicious.

Occasionally, for a special treat, as long as it was cleared by the staff, a parent would send their child's favorite food from which we were asked to prepare a meal. This was OK as long as enough ingredients were sent to serve the meal to all the kids. The fact that the staff had to clear it was comical, really; it's not like the parents were shipping in metal files to break their child out of Sing Sing. One of these parentally sponsored meals was my first introduction to the fluffernutter. If you don't know, it is simply a sandwich of marshmallow spread and peanut butter on white bread: the yin and yang of sweet and savory.

Now, I love white trash processed food as much as the next red-blooded American, but I can honestly say I had never heard of this concoction. Growing up a chubby I was never allowed peanut butter other than on saltines for a snack. Jelly was verboten. The only time I had the two together was digging my fingers in the jar of Goobers mixed peanut butter and jelly at a friend's house: processed food heaven. I would like to joke about how someone could get so excited about a fluffernutter, but of course it makes total sense. The foods of our home, of our youth, are dear, and are a touchstone of sorts. Especially, I imagine, if you are cooped up in a wilderness school 3000 miles from home, as this kid from New York was. So, we made those fluffernutters, and made them as best we could, which needless to say was not difficult. His thrill was inversely proportional to the difficulty, and warmed my insides.

Our two big splurge meals came, of course, at Thanksgiving and Christmas. I was advised not to really tamper with these, as they were tradition, and the kids loved them. For Thanksgiving it was the usual: turkey, (instant) mashed potatoes, gravy, and pie, which gave them another chance to freebase sugar. For the turkey, we ordered these quasi-spooky, partially boned-out turkeys. They looked like something you would see in a Dr. Seuss book: fully boned except for the legs. To carve you simply had to slice straight down. They almost belonged in a magic show as an illusion. Easy carving, for a big group, and everyone loved it.

The next big meal splurge was Christmas. The highlight of the Christmas meal was that each kid got his or her own Rock Cornish game hen! I was a kid in the 70s, so I have eaten my fair share of Cornish Hens, rumaki, and Bisquick sausage cheese bites. I even like Cornish Hens, but don't think of them as anything more than overpriced small chickens, which they are. But I was reassured: these little chickies were to be marinated overnight in a huckleberry salad dressing. What a delight. I think I threw up in my mouth a bit when they told me that.

I rarely ventured out of the kitchen except maybe to shoot the shit with my friends in admissions. But I did try to learn a bit of just what the hell the curriculum was, what their philosophy was, and what a kid had to do to have his parents send him to the middle of nowhere. My vast amount of experience making casseroles in no way qualifies me to judge the effectiveness of this program, nor do I profess to know all the ins and outs of the school. Relying 100% on hearsay, this school and others have helped a lot of kids. I just like to comment on the things that seemed, well, kooky as hell.

I'll bet you've heard that someone somewhere at some point has had to clean the floor with a toothbrush. I think I even saw it in Full Metal Jacket. But at the school, I saw this firsthand. The philosophy was that by doing this particular exercise, the student could see in all the lines of the floor, or grout, all of the various intersections in human relationships. This little exercise was given to students who would not open up and work on these complicated relationships. Um, OK.

Then, and this seems counterintuitive to the whole connotation of a "school" and it's bizarre school-like meaning, kids were not allowed to read too much. What? Did I hear that correctly? Yes. It seems that again, kids would rather read than go through some of that goofy New Age stuff, as well as painful self-discovery, so they were content to lock themselves away in their cabins and read. A lot. Where I came from this deviant behavior got you awards and good grades.

This is not to say that these kids were great little misunderstood young adults who wanted nothing more than to immerse themselves in a good book. After all, we had to lock up knives and yeast for a reason. As a staff member, I was warned never to have any interaction with a student unless the door was wide open, and even then it was preferable to have a witness present. In the past there had been false accusations of sexual harassment. Some of those little bastards would throw anyone under the bus in the vain hope that it might get them sprung.

A few would, indeed, do almost anything to get out of that place—even escape. Once they turned 18, the kids could leave of their own free will. They could simply walk away. Inadvisable given the location, but nevertheless. But if they were still a juvenile, they had to be found when they ran, as much for liability issues as for their own safety. How anyone got off that mountain is beyond me, but some did try. The staff called them "runners." Among some of the staff there was a perverse "The Most Dangerous Game" aspect to the whole shitstorm. "We got a runner!" one of the maintenance guys would say, and then Butch and Sundance and the rest of the Hole in The Wall Gang would saddle up in their trucks and head out to find the kid. Almost all the runners were found a mile or so away, having sadly underestimated the rocks and brush, as well as the Hole in the Wall Gang's prowess: most of the staff were game hunters in their spare time, after all.

What type of kid wound up in this little slice of heaven? Just like any normal school, there was a cross-section of personality types. There were the problem jerk off kids who needed a good throttling. There were the misunderstood, "woe is me, the world is cruel" types. There were some quiet, disturbed ones (the quiet ones are the worst) who were the reason the kitchen knives were locked away. There were many substance abuse cases. But at least in my short time there, in a woefully unqualified diagnosis, most were innocent victims of wealthy, too-busy-to-care parents. There was the son of a wealthy couple who had to be shown how to: a) tie his shoes, since he never had to, b) use a broom, and c) use a snow shovel. So the people who really needed the throttling, who needed the prune juice, the toothbrushes, and the neon cheese were the neglectful parents. These people who, after the horse—no, hell, the herd—was out of the barn, simply threw up their hands in despair and wrote a big fat check to this school for help. I did not like all of those kids. No. Many were assholes. But most I felt for, and went home at night and hit my own kids to keep them from winding up in a place like that. Kidding.

My time at the Shire was coming to an end. For me it was OK, in that I was close to opening (or so I thought) the albatross that was to be our future restaurant, Duke's Cowboy Grill. Also, I was getting sick of the touchy-feely New Age environment, and a few of the twits who made up the staff. I am far from a "spare the rod spoil the child" type, but I find it nauseating when kids call their teachers by their first names, and kids are encouraged "to find themselves." Finding yourself is really what expensive colleges, drugs, and alcohol are for.

It ended simply enough. I think two things accounted for this. First, even with my vast knowledge of food service and my fancy college diploma, I managed to miss making my food cost budget. I overspent every single month. I naively assumed the compliments and raves about the real food trumped the budget, but then very few things trump the budget. Second, my boss, Jean, actually the CFO of the school, came by one day and asked me if it made sense to have a manager at our school as well as one just miles away at our other sister school. I answered her truthfully: absolutely not. It made no sense. With ample staff in place, the menu at both could be the same and the manager could spend time in both places. This is what I would do. And this is exactly what Jean did. The other manager had been there for 10 years and thus had seniority, and was perfectly capable. I was shown the door. It was not all bad, however. I received a generous severance and was off to an entirely new career selling women the latest pantsuits.

SEVEN

....

THE FOUR SEASONS

After a couple of years we started to settle in to the rhythms of our town, and of the Idaho Panhandle. And for the first time in my life, I lived in a place that had four seasons, although they were not of equal length and were not the standard four seasons. Here they are effectively summer, fall, winter, and mud. Or, depending on the weather systems, they could be winter, cold winter, mild winter, and spring. Or, kind of dark, really dark, relatively dark, and light almost all of the time.

Nevertheless we settled in, and like everybody, our lives and events responded to the seasons. Spring, or mud season, means little teases by Mother Nature that a thaw just might actually come. Sun one day, snow the next. In fact, when we arrived it snowed on our wedding anniversary, May 6. As I was not yet fully acclimated to snow, I dutifully shoveled the snow from our apartment driveway using a dustpan. That was, until the recent college graduate who lived next door dispatched the snow in five minutes using his all-terrain vehicle with a plow attachment. We now own four snow shovels, one for each male in the family. Kim, in an unspoken mandate, has nothing to do with snow whatsoever, and our sons have a nifty habit of leaving their used shovels at the exact location where they finished using it, only for it to be buried over the season in many feet of powder. It's a numbers thing: this way we can find at least one shovel.

In those early days, our boys played T-ball and soccer. T-ball, if you have never experienced it, is at the same time cute and maddening. It's cute in that these little half pints are dressed in uniforms that, no matter how small, are always suffocatingly huge. Caps cranked to the last little nub, and even then, too large, shield their entire face. For us, this was small town living brought to life. The T-ball diamond was a block away, across the street from Dub's Drive-In, a local burger and shake shack. The field fittingly was called ... Dub's Field. Weather permitting, we would happily sit in lawn chairs and watch the tots do their best to make contact with the ball. Of course fielding was its own spectacle. For the kids to have a chance. the balls should have been the size of beach balls, with flashing lights and sirens. The best part was always the daisy pickers: those kids who summarily decided this game was bullshit and they were going to sit down, then and there. Sadly there were no daisies to be picked, but there *was* a shitload of dirt to make dirt angels.

Games became maddening when adults were involved. League commissioners, if there is such a thing, made sure that we played the full allotment of innings and played by the rules, with some coaches even arguing calls. I know. I know. Kids should learn the rules of the game. I would tell you that they have plenty of time for that later. T-ball-aged children have the attention spans of a cat chasing a shadow. If I had been commissioner, games would have been long enough for the kids to have one at-bat, and the parents to get a buzz out of their smuggled alcohol. Wait: for that last point I meant me. You see, to combat T-ball fatigue, I regularly smuggled wine in a Nalgene bottle to avoid the preachy stares from the true aficionados.

Spring, for our boys and for the majority of Sandpoint's youth, also meant soccer. (And for the parents, of course.) Saturdays during soccer season were blocked off entirely to allow for getting the kids dressed, transported and ready for games. Since soccer is so popular up here, we enjoyed this privilege twice a year, fall and spring. Soccer was a little more fun to watch, and of course shorter. Little tots, with socks pulled up to their groins and too-long jerseys, sporting shiny new cleats that would get exactly eight wearings or so, formed a rugby scrum that made its way in all directions. At some point the ball would squirt out and would possibly, just possibly, find the net. At one point during these years,

Jackson, our middle boy who was five or so at the time, decided to forego the rules as they are written, taking it upon himself to convert the game to tackle football. He tackled every single member of his and the opposing team, until his mother, mortified, had him removed and made him sit out the rest of the game. I thought he showed some promising open-field tackling skills.

For the adults, spring means an increase in activity around town. There is a risqué variety show in our old theater put on by a charity, and the possibility that one of the two local golf courses might open early. Normally this is the Elks course, a nine-hole course that very much resembles, well, a driving range with greens. If you are a player of my caliber, however, this course is indeed challenging as it is bordered closely on one side by railroad tracks. Even though they are not that close to the actual field of play, I have more than once hit shots that took flight, veered 90 degrees in a wicked slice, and clanged off of a boxcar. I would think for such a shot I would win some sort of prize, but no, golf can be an elitist sport.

Another spring event is the local art walk, put on by the art council. An event like this is, of course, not exclusive to our town. "Art" is set up in multiple local businesses, and patrons walk around town to view the pieces.

The "artists" show their "works" for sale and it is "catered" by the new local "caterer." Going to these shows often means staring at indecipherable canvases—or better, mixed media displays—while nibbling on crudités with ranch dressing and getting buzzed on boxed chardonnay, all the while trying to avoid air kissing the art matrons. I do not mean to knock boxed chardonnay. It is quite good in many cases, and the only way to get through these art shows.

In the big city open houses, or art fairs, or winery grape stomps, are often crowded, lively affairs. You may not know anyone, but there is likely to be people watching aplenty and a lot of activity. Small town events are largely under attended, no matter how much they are promoted. Part of this, of course, is due to the numbers: with a small population you're hard-pressed to get turnout as a percentage of the population, unless it's the annual cereal sale at the grocery store or livestock auction at the county fair. If your event happens to be on a weekend where another event competes with it, you can almost guarantee a small, depressing turnout.

But there is one way to attract at least a bit of a crowd: offer free stuff, like food or raffles of goodies during the event. In cities, this is rarely the sole reason to attend an event. In small towns, however, people show up, since the smarter of the herd do the math and figure out that their odds in a village our size are in their favor. The most depressing and annoying of these events, especially if you are a business owner, is the monthly Wednesday Happy Hour hosted by our Chamber of Commerce.

Here's the deal: once a month a local business is encouraged to hold an after-work happy hour (cleverly called the 5:01!) whereby the business offers free food and drink along with raffle items for fellow chamber members. The benefit for the business, they are assured, is that their business is spotlighted, and the other members are made aware of their services. Members will then pour money into that business like shit down a chute.

The reality of what happens is quite different. Carload after carload of hungry and thirsty chamber members show up at 5:01:30. They admire your wares or ask inane questions to show a modicum of interest in your business, all the while scarfing down the appetizers you made or purchased, along with the complimentary beer or aforementioned boxed chardonnay. They wait around until any raffle items have been raffled off and the food is gone. The bold will even pack a to-go plate to take home to their kids or their wheelchair-bound grandmother. You will be left with empty platters, empty pockets, and a sore rear.

Pretty much everywhere in the US, Memorial Day announces the beginning of summer. Not for us, though. Since Mother Nature still has a hold of our nether regions, no one barbecues or lies out in the sun, so Memorial Day hasn't transcended from its intended purpose into a commercial full-court press. No, summer waits to arrive every year on the 4th of July—you can set your watch by it. It seems appropriate, though, that summer is ushered in on our nation's birthday, replete with fireworks and a parade through our downtown core.

Parades, aside from those on national holidays that virtually no one else in the country pays attention to, are some serious shit in a small town. The whole town turns out. This day is quite literally Norman Rockwell brought to life. For the 4th of July parade, you have adorable kids riding their bedazzled tricycles. You have the antique tractor club doing curlicues in the street. You have the still-lingering war veterans from the local VFW. You have the annoying companies driving their trucks that you can see on the highway anyway, any time of year, in a thinly veiled marketing attempt. And for us, in the land of elk and moose and guns, you have the anemically filled ranks of the Sandpoint Vegetarians (anemic intended.) With their picket signs saying things like "The Garden of Eden was Vegetarian," the Sandpoint Vegetarians manage to keep on the parade route despite looking down their noses the entire time. One year their signs crossed over from pedantic to borderline offensive. At that point, I had an idea—just to annoy them, no other purpose, really—to form the Sandpoint Carnivores. Our picket signs would have said things like: "More Cow Now!" or "Pork to the People!" But the anger I felt from their preachiness receded in the intervening 11 months, and in my typical fashion, I was limited to just enjoying the sound of my own voice.

At sunset on the 4th, which at our latitude is half past nine, the fireworks begin all over Lake Pend Oreille. If you pick the right location you can see three or four shows, whether it's the public show put on by the Lions or Elks or some other mammal-inspired club, or private shows by homeowners. The best of these private shows are made up of fireworks procured at the local Native American reservations. Far better firepower sold there.

Summer here is fleeting, and adults pack as much fun into those days as possible. Like a time-lapsed photo of the President, you can actually see normally bright-eyed and bushy-tailed adults age over the course of eight weeks. The most arduous fun, almost requiring training for, is the Festival at Sandpoint. This music festival, featuring up-and-coming or down-and-outing musicians, takes place on our high school football field, which overlooks the lake and the mountains. The festival is general admission, allows booze and food to be brought in, and runs for two weeks in August. As cynical as I am, sitting under the stars, watching the moon rise over the mountains and listening to music: well, it's pretty special.

When the kids were small we hired college-aged babysitters for those summer months since there was no way on God's green earth we were watching them all day. We were happy to feed and clothe them, but we were not going to be submitted to that. For them, days meant going to the lakeside beach and playing on the swim platform. Think about that, adult reading this: summer days meant daily beach visits, ice cream, and swimming. Youth *is* wasted on the young. When we were forced to watch them, which was typically weekends, we came up with a variety of ways to keep them busy. My favorite was the obstacle course. These were loosely modeled on the old ABC sports program, *The Superstars!* I would design the course and usually the boys would have to do a half-mile or so of hopscotch, sink a few free throws, throw a football into a bucket while jumping on the trampoline, and do a few push-ups. Like parents and dog owners everywhere, the objective was simple: wear those little fuckers out.

As summer certainly starts on the 4th of July, fall is ushered in on Labor Day. As geese fly south, motorhomes and campers full of summer tourists also start their migration. Fall is magnificent, easily my favorite season of the year, and the shortest. For about a month or so, temperatures are perfect and leaves turn all of the warm shades. For a business owner, particularly in retail, fall is the time when you ask, "What the fuck just happened?" Especially if it is your first year in business. You are not prepared for the revenue door to slam shut so quickly. Retail owners go from working seven days a week in one of the prettiest times of year, to working seven days a week, short-staffed, just to make ends meet.

Halloween around our town is straight out of the movies. Leaves line the streets and sidewalks. The air is crisp. Pumpkins sit on porch steps, except for houses where those assholes who turn off their porch lights live. Since it is so Halloweeny in feel, one year early on I decided to really spruce things up. I intended to put tombstones in the front yard. After a bit of research I discovered that these were best cut from Styrofoam bricks and wired into the lawn. Easy.

You need to understand something here. I am not handy. I own one toolbox that is filled primarily with picture hangers missing their nails, a pair of adjustable pliers that I have never figured out how to operate, and a tape measure. The socket set I have is missing half of the sockets and the handle thing that you attach them to. For me to take on a project of this magnitude was unwise, but by this time I had told the kids how awesome (!) it was going to be, and like any project I undertake, I was optimistic early on. Armed with yellow-tinted Styrofoam (first hurdle), Krylon grey paint to overcome the yellow tinted Styrofoam, and a box cutter, I set out to make the stones. It took me all of 30 minutes to tire of this. As with all home improvement projects, I sabotaged myself by my utter lack of preparedness. I do not gather tools or measure, I forge ahead and wing it. Invariably I get pissed off, which only serves to make me hurry through said task until whatever it is, it looks like a child attempted it.

For the scary, scary tombstones, I made a stencil on whatever piece of cardboard was lying around at the time, most certainly a wine box. This, of course, had jagged edges—but hey, tombstones aren't ultra-smooth, especially in the days when Val Kilmer was a cowboy, which was what I was going for. What I didn't realize was that a box cutter was not the optimal Styrofoam cutter, because it shredded it hopelessly. No matter, I pressed on to the painting phase. Krylon claims their paint works on everything. I need to call them. It didn't really adhere to my yellow Styrofoam. I had to handle them very gingerly, lest the paint smear and rub off, which naturally it did. Originally I visualized the quaint Western gravestone sayings to be sort of *etched* into the foam. Roadblock. I was at a loss as to how to do this, and my patience was ebbing. So, sayings like "Here lies Lester Moore. Four slugs from a .44. No Les No More" I inscribed with a Sharpie. Except the ink didn't really get any purchase, sort of bleeding into the paint and shifting it around. Oh well. Second Sharpie application. After the second *etching* you really couldn't tell whether the words were written in the English language. When I was completely finished, and had dutifully impaled the Styrofoam at the bases with wire, I was ready to arrange my incredibly sad cemetery in our front yard. The only problem was that the bases were not deep enough to stand. That, and the wire was not cut long enough to sink into the ground. So with the slightest yawn of wind, they fell over. By this time I was done with this particular project, both literally and figuratively. I chose simply to make sure they were upright at dusk on Halloween. But I hadn't planned for rain. My tombstones didn't scare anyone except my wife, whose main fear was people would know she lived at this address.

Aside from Halloween, fall obviously ushers in the new school year. Here again we small town residents are a bit spoiled. Kids, unless they live out in the country,

walk or bike to school. They walk home. They stop off
for ice cream. They do not call or check in, unless they
are going to be late. Of course this takes some getting
used to, like keeping your car or home unlocked. But it
is nice and harkens back to a simpler time. If perchance
your child *is* late, panic does not set in. You simply think
that they stopped at a friend's house. Since everyone basically knows everyone else, it's not too hard to track
down your child. The best part of this comes when those
same adorable kids become annoying know-it-all teens.
Then you effectively have dozens of sets of eyes all over
the community. Our kids sometimes look at us like we
are wizards when we quiz them where they have been,
all the while knowing the truth.

If you ask my sons, the best part about fall is Thanksgiving. This is not too hard to understand, since it combines the great American pastimes of football and eating
until you are sick, but I'm surprised it trumps Christmas.
I am gratified it is so; I made a considerable and con-
scious effort to create a Thanksgiving my children would
remember fondly, a direct contrast to my own memories.
While my earliest memories of this holiday are positive,
those memories evaporate with my parent's divorce in
junior high. By the time I was in high school, and my
sister was doing her best to drink her way through LSU,
Thanksgiving meant there were two of us sitting down
to eat: my divorced mother, doing her best, and me. One
year as I was riding around our neighborhood on my
bike before the Cotton Bowl started and before we sat

down to eat, I noticed that almost every driveway had cars in it from guests and visiting family. At that point, I swore this holiday would be one surrounded by family and friends.

We start our Thanksgiving with the annual Turkey Bowl, a touch football game played at high noon, rain or shine, snow or sleet. We started this tradition with some good friends when all of the kids were small and slow. In those days the adults did not have to run very far at all, which was magnificent. In those days *in fact*, the adults even played. Now the adults dutifully suffer through the drafting of teams, but quickly "sub out" during the game to rehydrate with schnapps or beer. The Turkey Bowl outgrew its original location and has changed venue to the high school football field: War Memorial Field. The early start time allows us to clean up and ice injuries prior to the feast. Our dinners typically range from 10 to 20 guests. We move out the living room furniture in our old house and set up one long table where everyone can sit. Like good Americans, we eat with abandon. In fact, our boys have a disgusting white trash game of which they are quite fond: they weigh themselves before and after the meal for the "Net Weight Gain" award. Of course we are very proud. This parlor game has led me to make, on average, 15 pounds of potatoes for that meal alone. In some things at least, our sons are overachievers.

The snow flies in Sandpoint any time in November if we're lucky, and Mt. Schweitzer, the local ski mountain, tries to open around Thanksgiving. Sandpoint transitions then from its lazy summer vibe to ski town. Our boys have skied since they were young, thanks to their grandfather. Every year he bought them passes and gear, and took them skiing every Sunday. For this alone I suspect his mental stability. Early Sunday mornings, they would all pile into his tiny truck and eat cookies as they drove up to the mountain. He taught them how to get dressed, in which order, and how to properly take care of their skis. I wish he had taught me so I know how to get dressed. On most occasions, and for many years, Kim's mom and we would join and ski with them until lunch, foregoing church. Have you ever gone grocery shopping on Super Bowl Sunday? Sundays in Sandpoint are very similar. All of the good people are in church. We, however, were not. It was excellent; we basically had the mountain to ourselves. For a few years at least, I enjoyed skiing superiority over my sons, but that was not to last. They passed my abilities like a freight train. I was prepared for this, but I was not prepared for it to happen so goddamn fast. By the time our youngest was in the third grade, *he* would ski behind *me* to help pick up my skis once I wiped out. Blessedly, he was too young to realize how pathetic this was.

Winter also means that all of that light we enjoy in summer is sucked into the void. The sun sets around 4pm, give or take a few hours. Before moving to Sandpoint, I never considered Vitamin D. I didn't even know where it came from, or its purpose. Also, I never considered tanning. In Texas and California winters, afternoon jogs supplied enough cancer-causing UV rays to make everyone appear healthy. After a few winters here, with my complexion bordering on translucent and my moods base lining, I started eating Vitamin D like Pez. I happily tan, despite warnings from my dermatologist, who looks like a teenager and has perfect skin. I also now understand why Russians, Finns, Swedes and Danes drink so much. There is simply not enough booze to go around in the winter.

But during the month of December, our darkest month, the snow, cold, and dark combine to create a grand, festive holiday feel. Lights are strung in the trees downtown, store windows glow, and tree sellers pop up on gas station corners. Oops. I said "holiday feel." I did not say "Christmas feel." This is dangerous territory for Sandpoint, especially if you are in business. There are those who will boycott your business in a heartbeat if you or your employees have the gall to wish someone "Happy Holidays!" rather than "Merry Christmas!" I myself have suffered this injustice, enduring "Happy Holidays!" in several stores. How dare they wish me well?

Growing up on the Texas gulf coast, Christmas meant shopping for Christmas trees in shorts, hoping that the temperature might dip into the 50s; Turkey and Cajun-style oyster stuffing; and always *always* opening presents and celebrating on Christmas morning. We largely did not do anything meaningful on Christmas Eve, save the occasional Midnight Mass, unless you count my father having a number of cocktails, reminiscing fondly of the kale he ate in his native Germany, and, possibly due to said cocktails, forgetting to put the packages under the tree, choosing instead to hide them behind the couch. Christmas tree shopping is a bit different in our climate. If you are the adventurous sort, you will bypass the Christmas tree sellers and cut your own. Anyone can apply for a tree tag and venture onto public lands and secure their own tree. As this requires wherewithal and exertion, we have never done this. We choose to buy trees at a big box store with an orange logo, ignoring the irony that we are buying trees that have been cut down many miles away and shipped to a locale that has millions of them.

As far as Christmas the holiday, I am now a fire-breathing convert. I changed my ways when I married my wife. She and her family are solidly in the Christmas Eve camp and showed me the error of my ways. She is, after all, always right. Mona, Kim's mother, hales from Stockholm and is in charge of the holiday traditions. My wife learned to celebrate on Christmas Eve from that Swedish influence, since there, as in much of Europe, St. Nikolas visits children on Christmas Eve rather than Christmas morning. Whatever the reason, celebrating on the 24th has some distinct benefits. First, celebrating Christmas Eve in effect extends the eating and drinking one full day. Second, and this was crucial when our children were small, celebrating Christmas Eve solved the problem of waking up at an ungodly hour to open presents, since that task was already marked off. Third, we choose to ski Christmas mornings in lieu of church, assuaging our guilt with the promise of uncrowded ski runs. But the last reason is the best: celebrating on the eve is elegant and no one has morning septic tank breath. Following the Swedish theme, Mona furnishes a smorgasbord for family and friends, replete with Swedish food and drinks.

The menu typically consists of gravlax, that wonderful cured salmon with plenty of dill; *fågelbo,* a salad made of concentric circles of beet, potatoes, and anchovies, with a raw egg yolk center that is mixed together by the first person serving it; rare roasted beef tenderloin taking the place of the native Swedish caribou, served at room temperature with soft butter, rolls and Swedish hard bread; boiled shrimp, pickled with blanched onions, capers and bay leaves; traditional Swedish meatballs; *matjessill,* the ubiquitous herring; and the standout: Jansson's Temptation. This dish, beguilingly simple, is basically a scalloped potato made sublime with the additions of onions and anchovies.

We typically drink beer and aquavit, the Scandinavian moonshine. First we raise our beer glasses and toast a benign *skål,* all the while looking each other in the eye as it is custom to do so. After we have all had the chance to sample our way around our plates, murmuring with satisfaction as we do, the serious toasting starts with the song *Helan Går.* The song is legend. When Sweden's 1957 ice hockey team won the World Championships in Moscow, not all of the Swedish players knew the words to *Du gamla du fria*, the de facto Swedish national anthem, so the players sang *Helan Går* instead.

My Swedish vocabulary does not contain much more than the words Saab and Mats Wilander, so I believe loosely translated the words to the song go something like, "Drink drink drink, it's dark, we're cold, drink drink drink." Something like that. It hardly matters as the crowd shoulders on, mincing the words as they go. Toasts degenerate into women only, and then the men. If the stars are all in alignment, my father-in-law might throw in a special treat, a "dead bug," a toast used in the military to see who buys the next round involving getting on the ground and putting one's feet in the air like a dead bug. But this is a rare special treat.

EIGHT

···

COLDWATER CREEPS

"P ing!"

"Good afternoon! Thank you for calling Coldwater Creek! May I have the number in the pink box on the back of your catalogue please?"

"8176543."

"Thank you! Now may I have the number in the green box?"

"9883261."

"Thank you Mrs. Bedwetter! May I have your first item please?"

Only 15 short years after graduating from a prestigious academic institution, I was sporting my very own headset, complete with foam earpieces, working in the Coldwater Creek call center, taking phone orders for a woman's clothing catalogue company based in our tiny mountain town.

After I was laid off from the SMS, I assumed I would glide right into opening and operating the restaurant we had planned when we decided to move to Sandpoint. I was wrong. The process took much longer than expected, which included buying a building only to have it found unfit for occupation by the building inspectors. That was no problem, though; we sold it for a profit that was immediately sucked away, thanks to a clause in the loan penalizing early repayments. I am nothing if not consistent in my ability to do things the hard way. So there was about a one-year gap before we found a habitable building and broke ground, and I needed to find a job. Given my utter lack of transferrable skills, I figured: Coldwater Creek Call Center.

ColdWater Creek was a women's catalogue and retail store chain, founded and headquartered in Sandpoint. They flirted briefly with men's clothing, overpriced furniture, and a totally ill-conceived spa idea, but primarily they were a women's clothing retailer. Their catalogues always contained Northwest-style tchotchkes, gifts for that person about whom you hadn't given a single second of thought. At its zenith, when I worked there, the Creek, as it was called by locals, had hundreds of retail stores around the country. Its executives did wonderful things for our town, spending loads on our local charities.

The Creek was started about 20 years ago by a husband and wife team. It is a charming story of the owner biking the early orders to the UPS store for shipping, of growth, divorce, an initial public offering, and construction of a huge (for Sandpoint) facility. They eventually expanded into a fulfillment center on the East Coast and a large call center in Coeur d'Alene, about 45 minutes away, but they maintained a small call center in Sandpoint. I think they did this as a way to "give back" to Sandpoint when clearly the populace couldn't produce the numbers of qualified applicants necessary to staff a larger facility. The Sandpoint headquarters was a jewel, an actual corporate campus replete with a large warehouse, an auditorium, a fitness center, and a cafeteria, which was one of the better places to eat in town.

I figured this job was perfect. Taking calls from women, shooting the shit with them a bit, and then clocking out for the day. Easy. I told myself, I am personable, I can use a computer, and having been raised by a mother and an older sister, I knew a bit about fashion and I even appreciated it. In fact, as a boy I was an avid reader of Vogue and Harper's Bazaar. Mom had subscriptions to both and I regularly thumbed through them, hoping against hope to find the occasional picture of a naked breast. If an issue featured an article on "Breast Cancer Self-Screening" my eyes would light up: jackpot. (If Vogue and Harper's failed me, there was the ever dependable National Geographic for pictures of tribal women.)

However, there was one hurdle: a typing requirement, albeit a small one at 30 words per minute. This was a real problem, since I came perilously close to failing my seventh grade typing class as I was more fascinated with Mrs. Rohrs' auburn beehive that seemed capable of holding about 36 pencils than I was the keyboard. The first test, a warm-up, did not bode well: I completed 28 words per minute. I think a foreign-born child could type faster. But on the second test, with a laser focus and warmed-up digits, I turned in a blistering 33 words per minute.

I coasted through the rest of the interview and I was hired and assigned to a two-week training program with the other 15 new hires. The training was eight hours per day for two weeks. We were to learn a computer program called Ecometry, a cutting-edge yet cumbersome retail software. In two weeks our instructors were going to mold us into cheery, knowledgeable, call center operators worthy of the Creek. They were going to make us, in their words, creeky!

But first we had to learn the rules.

We were to punch in and out using a computer login. We were NOT allowed to punch in early. But if we were more than a minute late, we would be marked as "late" and a certain number of late logins were grounds for dismissal. Being late was considered exactly the same thing as not showing up for work at all. What? Despite my past experience with hourly employees and my homicidal thoughts toward no-shows, even I thought these policies were a bit extreme. A one-minute window? The calculus of "late equals a no show," however, was the real puzzler. During busy seasons, wouldn't it be better to have an employee show up 15 minutes late rather than not at all? Here's the real world effect of their math: one day I was stopped by a train on my way to work, a common daily occurrence here in Sandpoint. I sat there for seven minutes, watching the minute hand of my watch and its inexorable march past the twelve, the one, and the two. What did I do? You bet your ass. I pulled a U-turn and drove back home. Oh yes, I showed them: I gave up a full day's wages to make my point.

In the first few weeks, these rules made us arrive at work a bit early, gussy up in our headsets, and then watch the clock on the computer like a falcon watches a mouse. The clock turns. Punch! As time wore on, we instead arrived at the exact time, jogged to our desks, dumped our bags on the ground and frantically started the computer. We fumbled with our goddamn headsets and plugged the fucking things in. Just before the clock turned to the next minute we punched, placing all of our faith in the Internet connection.

We were allowed breaks, but they were scheduled for you. Breaks might only be an hour into a shift, so you then had hours and hours of phone calls to look forward to. It was totally random and maddening. Also, our hours were scheduled according to the season and the traffic flow, which was understandable. Some days were longer than eight hours, and in the slow periods some days could be woefully short. If you were scheduled in the evenings, you stayed as long as there were calls. Once the calls dropped off in the evening, our taskmasters in Coeur d'Alene who oversaw the Sandpoint office in the evenings would call us and shut the place down, often one operator at a time. It was a mini Powerball each night to see who got to leave early.

As employees, albeit call center employees, we were granted access to the health club and cafeteria, just like the corporate office executives and staff. But we were not equals with the corporate staff by any yardstick. Unlike our better-off cousins, if our time in the gym strayed too long, we beat it back to the call center like vampires at sunrise to punch back in for our time clock masters. To be realistic though, very few of our ranks went to the gym. Our average ages and bodies predicted this group would not know a crunch outside of something with Nestle stamped on it.

We also learned that calls would stream-in live to your headset as soon as you hung up a call. So, during the holiday season, this was every second of every hour of every day you worked. Literally as soon as you hung up the line, or rather pushed the disconnect button, there was the benign little ping! in your ear and you were back on the line. That little ping! was not so benign after a few hundred calls. It started to drive you a little batshit crazy. Also, you were not allowed to disconnect a call—this was a firing offense. Of course disconnects happened, sometimes honestly by pushing the wrong button, sometimes not so honestly. Despite how many hits my creeky attitude took, my Catholic guilt might be the reason I never purposely disconnected a call.

Finally, there was an appropriately termed "not on call" button. We used this button when we had use the restroom, or pretended we had to use the restroom, which was way the hell out in the warehouse and provided a much-needed walkabout. "Not on call" was also used when you were filling out some internal paperwork. It prevented an enthusiastic customer from dropping into your ear. Lest we use this button willy-nilly, its use was tracked by our superiors, along with our call numbers. We often pushed that button when trying to deal with the mind-bender that was a product return. All operators dreaded these return merchandise authorizations, or RMAs, but it truly put the fear of God in newbies like me. To do it properly, you had to open two separate product screens, return the item, add the authorization, re-order the product, and waive one part of the shipping. But what really made it devious was that we were supposed to not push the "not on call" button that I just said we actively used otherwise. The ideal was to keep one of the screens open in the background and circle back to it when the calls slowed. Right. We all pushed that button. Eventually we became adept enough to do these quickly without using the "not on call," but early on, product returns were enough to bring on what my dear old mother used to call the "G.I. shits."

When we arrived each morning for training, we traipsed through the call center where the vets were fielding real calls, on our way back to the classroom. We looked at them in awe since they had made it through training and were now chatting happily (or so we thought) with customers. What we didn't realize was that many of these folks had only "graduated" maybe two weeks earlier as the company was gearing up for the Christmas season. During those two weeks, we learned the software through repetition, all day, every day, repeating the same tasks, eventually building up to completing full orders. It was mind-numbing and we could only proceed to the next task when everyone understood.

The people in my graduating class of November '07 were a mixed lot. The majority were female, with ages ranging from the mid-20s to 65 or so. There was a handful of older ladies in our class who technology had not only passed by, but left them in its vapor trail. They had absolutely no chance of learning the cumbersome, many-stepped ordering system, but they persevered. I tried to help a couple of them. They eventually got it, but moved like glaciers. It was sad, but no surprise when they were let go the first week into live calls.

Eventually the big day came. No more practice. We were going live. Let's put this in perspective: this was not opening night on Broadway, or even opening night at Thomas Jefferson Elementary School. But it was nerve-racking. However, the crack call center curriculum and endless repetition took hold and we were able to fumble through those initial calls. The axe fell early for those who, despite 80 hours of training, displayed deer-in-headlights looks behind their computer screens. But the rest of us got into the groove. We reported to work toting those headsets that we had been assigned and gravely warned not to lose, since they cost $200 or some such bit of ridiculousness. Those cheap little pieces of shit headphones were churned out by the dozens in some remote part of the planet. And just like that, the Coldwater Creek Call Center graduating class of November '07 found itself staring into the maw of Christmas season.

To ensure that we were ready for Christmas, about two weeks after going live we were taped, or actually eavesdropped on by our leads. Leads were our superiors. My lead was a saucy little redhead who wore her leadership loudly and proudly. If she could have had a tiara, I have no doubt she would have worn it. Our other lead was newly promoted from our very ranks, after years of doing this. Years. She was not the field general that little red was, but was probably even more knowledgeable and very sweet. She commuted from God only knows where, in her weathered, brown, 1975 Oldsmobile Delta 88. Her husband, seemingly out of work, drove with her and dutifully slept in the car during her shift, passing the time with naps, smoking cigarettes, and bringing her Subway sandwiches.

For this particular eavesdropping session we were asked to sit right next to our lead and she plugged into our calls. We knew about it. But I still screwed it up. I did so because I felt the script we had been given to recite was horribly impersonal. Since my career to this point had been rooted in customer service, I made the de facto judgment to personalize it. I managed to conveniently forget how much I adored employees whom I had trained who ignored everything I said and did what they wanted. I also did not consider that a business whose metrics include the number of calls processed in a day might frown upon extra dialogue. So, after the sweetheart on the line gave me her info, I would say, in my best creeky tone, "How are you today?" Or better, I looked at where "my lady" was from and commented on that. (The Creek actually did call them "our ladies.") I changed a few other things, but time has benevolently erased my memory. It quickly became apparent that none of this personalized chatter was acceptable to my warden, plugged in to my left. I was made. Immediately after my first eavesdropped call, she had me push "not on call." This meant some serious shit. Little red dressed me down but good for straying from the script. I told her I thought the script was merely a guideline and my way was better. Not smart. Little Red told me to toe the line.

I did. I had to. I needed the job.

(Fast-forward. A designated eavesdropper listened in on our calls about once a month. We saw her coming from a mile away, so we were on our toes. By my second time, I had a perfect score. It was beautiful. I piled on the shit so high you couldn't see the horizon for the pile. I followed that script like a monkey. Every line was on time. And for bonus points (seriously), I commented on each item. "Oh Mrs. Jones! I just bought my wife that very same frock, and if anything it is prettier in person than in the catalogue!" Blech.)

Tuned up from our call monitoring, and with a few weeks' experience, we were ready for the holidays. Christmas season meant 10- to 11-hour workdays and what seemed to be millions of phone calls pouring into our headsets. And that's when it happened: the sea change in my attitude. My sunny, cheerful, creeky attitude was being worn down by the open fire hose of calls and the fuckwits on the other end of the phone. During the blur that was the Christmas season, we fielded lots and lots of calls trying to help lots and lots of clueless husbands hoping that they were buying the right thing from the right catalogue. We helped impatient women who had waited too long, given in, and ordered multiple items for relatives to be sent to multiple addresses. We tried our best to coax the right information out of the confused so we could place a one-item order. We took orders from Canadians who shipped their wares to relatives in the US in order to avoid the few bucks that was the VAT. And we dutifully explained the differences in sizes between an XL, a 2X and a 3X. There were a lot of those calls.

As we got closer to the actual holiday, we received updates from our superiors on the date we could guarantee our customers that their precious, under $20 stocking-stuffer! of polar bear pajamas would make it to their loved ones on time. As we got really close . . . I did the math. Were they serious? We could guarantee that they would arrive on time? In what time-space continuum? Of course, I understood. The majority would arrive on time. Some wouldn't, and these dolts had waited too long anyway. If we told them no, we couldn't guarantee on-time delivery, they were likely to hang up. We'd probably blame the shipping company regardless. So, we maniacally told every single customer that as late as the 22nd of December that yes, their orders would arrive in time for Christmas. Because I believe that is what UPS or FedEx or whomever told us. Now you and I both know that is utter bullshit. You cannot go into your doctor with a sprained ankle and have him guarantee, if pressed, that you will be as good as new. He might not even guarantee you'd live. Doctors don't guarantee anything other than that you are going to wait very long to be seen, and pay a considerable fee for their services. But we guaranteed on-time delivery. It was Christmas Craps.

As fun as the pre-holidays were, post-holiday calls were drastically shittier. It's not hard to imagine why: immediately after the holidays, we got calls from those very same people complaining that their slippers hadn't arrived on time and where were they? We then tracked their packages. Even a few short years ago, package tracking was not what it is now. Yes, we used the Internet, but it involved many more hoops to jump through than it does now. These calls droned on until we were able to verify what part of the country their package was in. A few days later, the 6th or 7th circle of hell arrived. I am rusty on my Dante, so I'm not sure which applies here. It was not tantamount to being chewed forever by the devil, but it was certainly worse than the punishment the usurers received.

Product returns. The dreaded multi-screen circus. All of those ill-advised purchases and incorrect sizes were coming back in droves. Or, cousin Beulah, who hated what she received, called to return her item on the down-low. "Yes ma'am, we can return that and your cousin won't know."

In those days right after Christmas, almost every call required opening two screens, scratching down RMA numbers on a notepad to insert in the other screen. It sucked. Our days were filled with this nonsense. The afterglow of Christmas is quickly sucked out of your system when you work in a call center after the holidays. Unless you were Mason. Mason matriculated with me in the class of late November '07. He was the guy who would ask a million questions concerning break times and lunch times, down to the last scintilla of information. In meetings Mason would ask questions that only applied to him and no one else in the room. "I have a problem working Saturdays. Those are the only days that I get to see my kids." Way past the point of decorum, well past the point of someone remotely giving a shit. At night, rather than waiting for the call to go home from our superiors, he would actively call them, effectively doing the most annoying thing in life, something you learn in kindergarten never to do: cutting in line.

The best part, of course, was that he was completely oblivious. It shouldn't have been a surprise that Mason's solution to all of these returns was to simply tell the customer to use the return form in the box and process it through the mail. Like hanging up on a customer, this was verboten. A serious offense. But he was comfortable in the fact that the beehive hum of so many voices drowned out his trespass. At this point in the joyous season, I entertained thoughts of wrapping the phone cord around his neck.

Soon, however, the call center settled to post-holiday normalcy. This was great, except for the fact that as the calls slowed, the hours slowed as well, and our head count slowly dwindled. But we were in for one last treat: the after Christmas clearance sale, a furious week-long period where we had the pleasure of not only dealing with nagging customers, but enduring the cheap ones on top of it.

Jessie and I weathered the holidays and the clearance sale together. Jessie was not in my graduating class; I think he was a month or so my senior. Jessie was a helluva a nice guy. He was an overweight, self-taught computer wizard. He was trying to secure a job in the IT department and was using the call center as a means to get his foot in the door. It was tough sledding. Like me, he hated the call center. Whenever we could we sat next to each other, rolling our eyes in unison as our mouths spewed wax museum fakeness.

Eye-rolling had many levels. By this point I could tell within a few seconds what type of call this was going to be. Simple order? Easy: very little eye-rolling. But if the woman on the other end fumbled with the customer number, or started asking questions immediately, before we could get our crucial information, eyes really started to roll. If the customer on the other end started with "I'd like to return six or seven items," our eyes rolled spasmodically, eyebrows arched in a way that would make Jack Nicholson proud. Depending on our mood, we would slam the mute button and pantomime "FUCK!" in an almost whisper.

Occasionally, Jessie and I would have races to see who could record the speediest call. It was fantastic. I think my best time was about 23 seconds beginning to end. That was fast, if you consider that we had to take payment as well. Jessie, however, posted an alarming 21 seconds that might be the fastest call ever. Any attempt or preamble at customer service during such calls went sailing out the window.

I still remember the call. Jessie had luck on his side as this woman needed exactly one item and was probably sitting in her recliner, clutching both her catalogue and her credit card. We had been competing against each other all morning, to pass the time. When the call came in, he spoke so fast that I could barely understand him, and I knew what he was supposed to say. If he had been monitored, I don't think the post-eavesdropping session would have gone well. But to me, sitting in my cubicle, it was pure genius. His fingers flew over the keys like a savant. It was, simply, call center beauty.

Just prior to the big sale, since the calls had slowed down, we could actually chat before some asshole customer popped into our ears. (It really pissed us off when a customer ruined a perfectly good conversation.)

Normally, Jessie regaled me with tales of his wife. He told me she was drop-dead gorgeous and had an insatiable sex drive. That, and every day she packed him gourmet lunches with sex notes in it. Obviously, he was delusional. I loved the guy, but he was no looker. I know, I know, looks don't matter to women. They are not as shallow as men. But I mean come on. Also, I have never never never never met a woman who was gorgeous and horny. Oh wait: gorgeous, horny, and married. That last part normally eradicates one or both of the previous qualifiers. Not that a woman like this didn't exist; scientists didn't think the coelacanth existed either.

I never met Jessie's phantom bride, but I am able to give proof of two of her attributes. Yes, she did pack him great lunches, this I saw. There were sandwiches of roasted peppers, sausages and smoked mozzarella. There was freshly made hummus with naan. Bagels with lox. And then one day Jessie handed me a note from his lunch box. His wife wrote something to the effect that she couldn't wait until he got home so she could, well, fellate him. Of course, he could have written this and packed his lunch himself. But for everyone who has ever had a dream, I refuse to believe that.

The time for the yearly sale arrived. There were two caveats to the sale that were guaranteed to cause us misery. First, not everything was available and on sale. Only certain items listed on the website were available. Confusion about this was inevitable. Second, and this was the killer, was that if someone purchased the same object, say, two weeks prior, at the time it was not on sale, they could call in during the sale and get a refund for the difference. My hat went off to the company for this policy as it cemented goodwill among their audience. They figured the number actually calling in to do this borderline nefarious thing would be small. And they were right. But for us it was huge. Creating this refund in the system was terribly problematic, worse even than a dreaded return. It drove us almost homicidal that these people were getting away with this! I could barely conceal my contempt for them. Both Jessie and I were pretty good at delivering speedy calls, but when I got one of these shameless assholes on the phone I slowed down to a just-out-of-kindergarten pace. My own little pound of flesh.

A few days into the sale, with my feet propped up on my desk, my keyboard stretched to the limits of its cord and lying in my lap, I had an idea how to turn this shit show into a bit of fun. My cubicle was at the far end of the call center near the wall, well away from prying eyes. I taped together a few open manila folders with strapping tape procured from the shipping department and created a rather unscientific-looking chart. This allowed me classify the calls I was receiving.

It was not hard to categorize these calls after you had taken 200 or so. During the conversation, the moment I was able to deduce which type of call it was going to be I dug my heels into the linoleum and rocketed my chair across the floor to quickly make a hash mark on my chart that was now masking-taped to the wall.

The calls basically fell into these categories:

Uptight white New York/East Coasters: These were quickly identifiable by their nasally accent, impatience, and superior attitude. Complete Bitches.

Clueless hillbilly southerners: Again, the accent gave it away. But in contrast to their northern counterparts, who were all business, these gals had that stereotypical slowness to them. Halfway through these calls, I wanted to shove a letter opener through my soft palate and end it all right there.

You-will-never-fit-in-that-so-for-the-love-of-God-please-don't-order-it types: These were the gals who, upon being informed that we were out of their size, decided to see if they could sausage themselves into something smaller. Most times the conversation went like this:

She: "Do you have that in a 3x?"

Me: No ma'am, we only have a 2X and an XL available."

She: Pause. Sigh. "I'll try that."

Me: "Which one, please?"

She: "I'll try both."

This got under my skin for a couple of reasons. First, I thought this was an exercise in futility. Second, I was likely to be the poor bastard who, in a few weeks would have to process the return.

<u>**Clueless shopping addict out to save a few bucks**</u>: This customer received the catalogue and made a beeline for the rotary dial phone. When this person called, she had no fucking idea what was on sale or not. All she saw was the word "sale" on the cover of the catalogue, and she sprang into action. These customers typically went item by item through the catalogue asking me to look it up in the system to see if it indeed was on sale. In 99% of the cases it was not. As I neared the now inevitable aneurism, the customer would either give up with a heavy exhale, or order something else that likely would not fit, nor be what she wanted. It would then sit in the closet, or, you guessed it: be processed in a few weeks for return by a sad sack like me wearing a goofy foam padded headset.

<u>**Cheap motherfuckers with no sense of pride**</u>: These were the customers I mentioned before. They had the item, likely purchased for Christmas at full price, and wanted a refund for the difference. Or, even better, they received this item as a gift and wanted to get a refund or gift card for the difference. I wanted to kill these people. Or have them killed. It was that simple.

By the end of the sale, my handy spreadsheet was filled with tally marks. I forget who won the contest, but it's really not important, is it? The joy is in the doing.

After the sale, and between holidays, call volume became painfully slow. Schedules were a maximum of a few hours for the dwindling number of survivors at Call Center Sandpoint. The once-bustling center was inhabited by a few souls, with the majority of cubicles empty. Without any adrenaline, it became even more mind-numbing than normal. Fortunately, Kim and I were in the final phases of obtaining a loan for our soon-to-be restaurant. Mercifully I packed up my cobalt blue "Happy Holidays from Coldwater Creek!" Christmas bonus mug and quit.

And Jessie? He eventually found that job with the IT department, but quit a year or so later to do his own IT consulting. I still see him occasionally tooling around town in his blue truck with dual white racing stripes down the hood, and I think of the times we had, shoulder-to-shoulder, selling women's clothes. And then I wonder how his wife is doing.

I took one call just before I quit, from my hometown of Houston, Texas. The last name was one I recognized, and was highly unusual: Veselka. I had an English teacher in the eighth grade with that very name, so on a lark I played the name game and hit pay dirt. It was indeed my teacher's wife. After I hung up, I backtracked through the years to where I was now. I looked at my reflection in the desktop monitor and thought: at what point did I make the wrong turn? Was it obvious? Here I was, sitting in a call center in a small town in northern Idaho taking phone orders for the latest pantsuit. I reassured myself that Kim and I had simply stepped off the treadmill and chosen a different, slower lifestyle and a better upbringing for our kids, but that kind of epic rationalization does have its limits. If Robert Frost had been alive then, and I encountered him on the street, despite his grandfatherly appearance I might have punched him in the throat.

NINE

···

THE DRAG 'EM INN

I thought it was a good idea. I thought it was a good idea in much the same way that Coke thought it prudent to change an already great recipe, and maybe in the way that Garth Brooks thought it was a good idea to break away from his successful country career, change his hair, create a pseudonym, and launch a new career. Well, at least *he* had a well-paying other career to fall back on.

The idea, of course, came to me while Kim and I were contemplating our move to Sandpoint. I decided to leave behind my utter failure as a steam cleaner salesman and dive back into the restaurant business. Knowing Sandpoint and the pathetic lack of career-type jobs for someone of my skill set, I realized that the only way to make real money was to start my own business, a restaurant being the obvious, perilous choice. Just writing these words makes me think I should have my head

examined now for what I did then, just to make sure I
don't, at some point, decide to stick my tongue in an
electrical outlet. I also had the disease that most in the
restaurant industry have and was jonesing to get back in.

How did I forget that I had opened a restaurant before, with a dear friend and extremely capable chef, and
it had been a huge undertaking for two people? Is it akin
to forgetting that childbirth is like passing a bowling ball
and then happily deciding to have more kids? Opening a
restaurant entails a mountain of paperwork, permits and
jumping through hoops, not to mention the fact that
restaurants are very labor intensive—lots of moving
parts—so they require babysitting all the time and great
people to help it run. Nevertheless my fear of not suc-
ceeding stared down my fear of failure and won, if that
makes any sense.

But you can only get to that promised land if you can
raise enough cash to get the place running. I have said it
before: I am miserable at asking investors for money.
And it takes a special type of person to pour money into
a restaurant; only in rare circumstances do they hit it so
big that they make the owners rich. In most cases the
investor is some rich bastard who wants special treat-
ment when he walks in the door. For them, owning a
restaurant makes them part of the team without having
to clean the grease trap, or plunge the toilet after some
old farmer lays waste to it after lunch.

Unlike our restaurant expansion plans in California,
we were able to actually find investors here, and they

appeared to have all of their faculties. But the ball would not have started rolling without an old college friend of Kim's dad. I choose to believe, wrongly I'm sure, that his initial investment came from confidence in the project rather than charity. In any case, his princely support lent credibility to the project, and armed with some whiz-bang spreadsheets that a banking friend prepared, we were able to convince a few locals to join the ranks.

We did not raise the entire amount we needed. No, that would have been like asking for a unicorn. But we did raise enough to be hopeful of getting a loan for the rest. Thankfully the Small Business Administration is willing to loan money to almost anyone. On financial *projections* no less! Of course it's not that simple, you do have to write a business plan, demonstrate your proficiency at tying your shoes, and be able to construct sentences. I overstated that for humorous effect, but it really was painfully simple to be lent a whole lot of money. You do have to complete one minor detail: you have to personally guarantee the loan. At the time you are signing your house away, your butt puckers only slightly because you are certain—certain—that if you do everything in your power this cannot fail.

Our first move was to purchase the perfect building in the perfect spot. It was a former paint store that, like many businesses in our town, was a former residence. It was on a lot with available parking and the lot itself was on the edge of downtown and passed by about 15,000 cars on their way through and out of town. We spent thousands of dollars on some nifty architectural plans. Things were rolling! And then we had the place inspected. It was not fit for habitation. We couldn't even burn the goddam place down—I know, I tried. I am not confessing here to attempted arson. We actually asked the fire department to burn the place down in a training exercise. I'm not sure why they wouldn't do it, but it sure seemed like a bad sign. Not to worry, we sold it relatively quickly to a savvy investor who held on to it for a bit and made a nice return. The added bonus to this experience was that we also paid a hefty early repayment penalty on this little loan. On to Plan B. The Dragon Inn.

The Dragon Inn—*"The Drag 'Em In!"* to the locals, was another old as fuck former residence that had been turned into a business on Highway 200 leading west into Montana. It was one of two Chinese eating adventures in Sandpoint. Actually, it sits in Ponderay, Idaho, the phonetically spelled town that self-proclaims "The Little Town with the Bright Future!"

My response the first time I drove past what was to become Duke's Cowboy Grill was something like, "No way I'd open a restaurant there. Too far out of town. Off the beaten path." I think I even said that out loud. But you know what? Over time, as no properties within reason became available, and because we needed to purchase land rather than lease as a means to qualify for the SBA loan, desperation and hope started to work their magic. It will be a roadhouse! A little out of town, sure, but I mean really, it's only one mile! Just like a Texas roadhouse! My rose-colored glasses allowed in just enough light to imagine my roadhouse: a huge deck for summer, spacious grounds for kids to run around, strung-up lights . . . we could landscape . . .

Lesson #1: As the saying goes, trust your gut, because desperation and hope are motherfuckers that will cause your mind to convince you of something that is not right.

Lesson #2: Big grounds mean big upkeep. I should have learned this already since we purchased our large, rambling house. I have now made this mistake twice and it's a gift that keeps on giving: you pay first for all the land itself, and later on all of the upkeep.

At least it was a better location than our California restaurant that was located on El Camino Real. That place had about five square feet and was wedged nicely between a stained glass studio and school and a pornography store (pre-Internet!) whose owner kept at least two dozen cats, and for recreation, played miniature golf on the 18-hole course he created out of papier-mache.

Once we bought the place, next came the renovation process. This part was fantastic fun—conceptualizing interiors, sourcing equipment, acquiring décor pieces, and thinking up witty slogans for T-shirts. But it was also fraught with anxious moments, as potentially any hammer strike could yield mountains of asbestos that would require fixing, and steal away money that we didn't have.

The first of these happened on day one. Yes. Day one. The deck attached to the side of the building fell off. Not on its own, but with only two bolts loosened. Not so bad really, as we were going to demolish it because— surprise!—it appeared to be as rickety as shit. The bonus was that the deck took with it a gas line about as big as an adult's forearm, and the whole highway had to be closed down in both directions. It's kind of reassuring, or comical really, to see our police and fire departments respond to anything more than a stray cat or the local drunk hitting his girlfriend. They respond with over- whelming force because they are just dying to get some action. I'm not saying this didn't require highway clo- sure, but seriously, it looked like the FBI sealing off the David Koresh compound many years ago.

Here's the thing, though: I didn't really see it. I just saw it on cell phone photographs. After all of this hap- pened, our contractor went to the bank where my wife worked and told her about it. This is the same contractor of Wednesday Breakfast Club fame. This is the same bank where our current banker, who hired my wife years ago, was the president. We also bought his house when he left for greener pastures. Small towns are incestuous places. Knowing that I might open an artery upon hear- ing the news about the deck collapsing and creating a potential disaster, Kim forbade him from telling me. I found out well after the fact via the photos, once all was back to normal.

This was by no means the last of the "circus comes to town" atmosphere of the remodel. If you've been through a remodel of a house or kitchen you know from where I speak. Delays and overruns are the norm, but the normal remodel typically doesn't include a guy showing up to retrieve his bat repellers. This was the first I had heard that such a thing existed. One day, not too far into the remodel, a somewhat wild-eyed, alabaster-haired gent showed up to remove the objects he used for repelling bats in the attic of the former Drag 'Em Inn, implying that they were quite valuable. They were, in fact, Renuzit Solids. The 70s-era room deodorizers. The exact flavor eludes me. Our town's version of Dr. Emmett Brown claimed that these were the silver bullets of bat prevention; it seems the smell drives them away. Doing our best not to show how crazy he appeared to be, we told him that there weren't any Renuzits to be found, nor was the oscillating fan that he used to spread the 70s-era smell. He became outraged, threatened to involve law enforcement (that would have been worth it), and went away. But he was right about one thing: the many inches of guano in the attic proved that there indeed were bats living at the Inn at one time. Of course, we already had those suspicions when we removed the stove exhaust hood to clean it and found one entombed in grease in the motor.

The entire period of the remodel I walked around on eggshells. It's a common axiom that to start a business, especially a restaurant, you need to have large reserves of working capital. If doing a remodel, have plenty in the bank as those damn things get expensive quick. Since we didn't have large cash reserves, I was a mess the entire time. My anxiety was not unfounded. First it was the deck, and then came the exhaust hood. One day late in the remodel, our contractor told me that the exhaust hood, a comically tragic piece of shit that was manufactured back when people were five feet tall, was not up to code and had to be replaced. Crap. We got an estimate from our "equipment specialist," a rheumy-eyed gent, with one of those eyes being a lazy one, who was about 150 years old. (Some on our crew were also convinced that this same gent tipped off the county health folks to get another equipment sale.) Exhaust hoods are expensive, and if you are not used to ordering one, there is some tricky lingo about return air and a bunch of other jargon associated with them. So, in this age of the Internet, I ordered one on eBay. Here is why that is not an optimal plan: going by the engineer's estimate on cfms (Greek to indicate suction power, *cubic feet per minute*), I ordered one that would easily lift a hairpiece off of your head. In the hot summer months, it also sucked out every bit of cool air from the Paleolithic-era air conditioner, and in the winter, sucked out every scrap of heat in the building. This was not a small problem. Not only were customers freezing their asses off in the winter, but we were paying huge electric bills for the privilege of powering a fan that simultaneously sucked out air that we paid to have in there.

Thankfully, Kim, who has always been the stable one, steadied my nerves and kept track of loan disbursements, among other things. Obviously we fed and clothed the kids during that time since they are still alive now, but I have no memory of it. Perhaps being so mentally checked out led to another smart decision: we put a down payment on a puppy whose arrival would coincide with opening day, give or take a few weeks. To say this was ill-advised would be kind. We were going to throw a black Labrador puppy into the spin cycle that was our lives. I was assured, however, that labs thrive on contact and that he would happily sit in my office at work. I think it was the Tooth Fairy who assured me of these things. Of course it was not just any dog, it was the son of the dog owned by our banker, who hired Kim, sold us our house, and introduced us to our investors. Of course. If the fact that the dog snared a can of sardines off the shelf in my office, opened it with his teeth, emptied it and polished the interior to a fine sheen, leaving no trace in the office or in his mouth is any indication, then yes, he did splendidly well hanging out in my workspace.

As the remodel neared completion, it was time to turn my attention to staffing. This proved to be a nightmare. In the Bay Area, a newspaper ad—how charming!—would lead to literally stacks of employment applications. But this was small town 'Ho, where the pool of talent is a puddle. To make matters worse, we were smack dab in the middle of the housing bubble.

Thanks to that and some well-placed magazine articles touting the area's beauty, everyone and their brother were leaving their normal jobs to become a realtor or a contractor.

Two weeks removed from opening, we were *maybe* half-staffed. Maybe. If we were half-staffed, all of those positions were counter positions, not valuable cooks. The cooks I interviewed and eventually hired were a frightening bunch, the veritable island of misfit toys all in one spot. There was the "cook" who, within one month, had a sexual harassment accusation against him, and would have had more if the women in question had even a morsel of sense to realize what was going on. There was the gal who claimed that cigarette smoke helped her combat onion fumes, hence her numerous cigarette breaks. They were eye therapy. Our two starting bussers had a combined IQ of maybe six.

Staffing interviews usually went something like this:

Me: Why do you want to work here?

Them: I need a job.

Me: I see a gap in your work history. What have you been doing?

Them: I just got out of jail.

Me: (startled, but keeping an uncomfortable grin on my face) Really? For what?

Them: Meth possession, but I've given it up.

Me: Next.

And then there was my prize hire: a former convicted felon who, after a week's work, "allegedly" broke into our very restaurant to steal the cash drawer. Months later he moved into the house of a local doctor who was out of town at the time, and lived there for a short time, pretending to be the owner of the house. Please. I can't make this shit up. One hire turned out to be a godsend. Ignacio, Nacho for short, was originally from Guatemala but hailed recently from Arizona where he had worked in real kitchens like The Olive Garden. He was a fireplug of a guy who could really cook. He ended up riding out the storm with me, eventually becoming the manager and my right arm.

Despite the fact that new hires were trickling in slowly, the opening date was fast approaching and it was time to begin training at Duke's Cowboy Grill. The concept centered around the three pillars of Texas cooking that I grew up eating: authentic BBQ, no-beans chili, and Tex-Mex specialties. The décor included tacky kitsch that poked good-humored fun at the Texas and Western stereotypes. Hubcaps framed a Texas flag painted on the ceiling. Our electrician strung light ropes around and through the saddles that were chandeliers. A TV ran nonstop spaghetti western movies. We converted a horse trough into a sink to wash your hands, the booths were from an old diner, and the sweet tea was served in quart-sized mason jars.

Originally, I budgeted for one full week of employee training and one week of dry runs. These are relatively common in the restaurant industry, whereby you practice on people for free, working out the kinks. Early on the employees are the lab rats, and then you graduate to invited guests, the contractors and hired hands who worked on the project, and in bigger cities, charities that can even charge their patrons, make some money on the deal, and lend a festive snobby air to the event. Who doesn't want to be part of the in-crowd at the new hot spot? But due to construction delays we weren't able to hold to this schedule. Another reason we weren't able to hold to my training and practice schedule was that one investor was pushing to open the doors, due to the fact that he had invited friends and family to the opening of "his" new restaurant and wanted it to be open. Looking back, it comes as no surprise that servers learned to run and hide when he and his family came in to eat. Literally. They scurried like church mice. Of course, I did too, on occasion.

I had a good idea of recipes, but had no time to battle test them. This was especially troublesome in a part of the country that did not know that authentic BBQ wasn't heavily sauced, Southern cornbread wasn't sweet, and generally had an aversion to food that was spicier than Malt-O-Meal. One of our new cooks was the wife of a local electrician. She was Central American, surly as hell, and in charge of making fresh salsa. The day would start and she would say, "Cut cut?" I would say "yes," and then she proceeded to take a case of tomatoes, put them in our industrial strength, one horsepower food processor, and turn them into so much tomato borscht. Exhibit #1 on the merits of practice and dry runs.

Somehow we limped onward through our shortened training period, and opening day came with seemingly decent reviews of our food; but of course, the reviewers were friends, and they ate for free. Unlike some small towns perhaps, Sandpoint has a decent number of restaurants—too many, really. Some are very good, most are average. Despite the relatively large number, once the population sees the "Opening Soon" sign for a new place, they mark their calendars. The honeymoon period just after opening is a steamroller. In cities, at least among those in the know, you simply don't go to restaurants right after opening. It takes weeks for the best, and months for the others to get their feet under them and correct mistakes. Not so in Sandpoint. It seems that every soul and their distant relatives show up opening day.

Opening day, I arrived as I had all week at 5am. Kim took the week off from the bank to help out. She effectively was the front of the house manager and I was managing the kitchen staff. Farrah Fawcett, from my days managing the Snowpeak School, was our morning cook and provided a much needed beachhead. This was a pretty serious job, since Farrah was in charge of smoking all of the briskets for dinner and ribs for lunch. When you have a restaurant that used to be a home and then a Chinese restaurant and reputed brothel, you have the walk-in refrigerator and prep space located in the basement, while the smoker and cooking line is upstairs. Translation: Farrah had to hump hundreds of pounds of meat up the stairs each morning.

Lunch went off well. We were busy but not overly so, and we had not advertised that we were opening. In the industry, this is known as a soft opening. You open up, to probably fewer people, but again, it gives you the opportunity to correct mistakes and prepare for bigger crowds. The dinner shift came on at 2pm and we got ready for dinner. My nerves were like so much piano wire. But we were at least fully staffed, with Nacho cutting barbecue and two other cooks handling the rest of the line. I was to help call out orders and coordinate with the front of the house.

In my experience, a dinner rush, at least those not made up by senior citizens, starts at 5pm at the earliest. Not that day. Four pm. When we opened the doors at 4pm there was a line queued out the door and down the newly installed wheelchair ramp. Cars and trucks filled the ample parking lot and were parked well down the highway shoulder. It looked like a revival meeting. And that line never stopped. Our fancy point of sale system, which consisted of touch screen monitors attached to a printer on the cooking line, was too damn fast. We would have been better off writing tickets by hand using our toes. At least that way the kitchen might have had a chance.

I built the concept around quick service, like say, a Chipotle, where you order, grab a drink, and wait at a table for your food to be ready. When it was, a coaster the cashier had given you would light up. Chips and salsa (cut cut!) were available in the meantime in a restored

'55 Chevy truck bed complete with working tail lights and a dry-ice fueled exhaust to simulate smoke. After you snacked on chips and salsa, we then buzzed your coaster and you picked up your food. Two problems here. First, this relatively common concept in some cities was, to our clientele, straight out of the Jetsons. Second, the menu that was written in chalk on old doors hanging on the wall served to cause ordering confusion. It was all just too much for a new operation to keep up with, and my insistence on some salads and burgers on the menu made timing and completing orders more difficult.

So at 4:01pm the tickets started to come off the printer. Then the ticket line was full. Then the tickets were hanging double on the ticket line. Then the printer spooled over the back, pooling orders on the greasy, brisket juice floor, which we didn't notice since we were so far "in the weeds." (Instead of "the weeds," that restaurant feeling for being completely overloaded, the French say "the shit" and I couldn't agree with them more.) Then, *then*, we started running out of food. Twenty-five racks of ribs. Pork butt. Brisket. We madly started sending runners to negotiate customers into another meal, with $25 coupons good for their return visit. Finally, we were out of all our food. All of it. By 6pm.

One of our food salesmen sent his know-it-all district manager to help out for opening night, I guess to show they care. After our night came to a quick end he asked, "Have you done this before? Are you new to the restaurant business?" I was too shell-shocked to respond. After we closed the doors bright and early, we made an emergency order with our grocery company located in Spokane. Since it was Saturday and no delivery trucks were available, Kim and a friend rented a U-Haul and drove the massive order down themselves. Our banker, happy to help, and happy for us in what looked to be a huge success, unloaded it for us. And on we went.

I'd like to say that the next day was as smooth as silk. Not quite. In my desperation to get off to a good start, a few weeks earlier I had taken a catering order for 150 people to be ready at 5pm that second day, coinciding with dinner. Growing up, my mother, a staunch Catholic, would invoke, "Jesus, Mary, and Joseph!" when things got really dicey. Jesus alone was not enough: you needed all three. This was one of those times. Oh, we got the catering order ready. And in plenty of time, too. But how do you store food for 150 if your ovens and other cooking surfaces are filled to capacity with food for regular dinner service?

Light bulb moment.

You put all of the food—in this case, ranch beans and brisket in aluminum serving containers— on the racks in the rotisserie smoker. These are the same shitty serving trays you use at Thanksgiving for turkey. But here's the deal. They are not really that sturdy. I'm not sure why, I skipped physics. But as we were removing them from the rotisserie, they folded up like deck chairs. *Gallons* of beans spilled into the bay of the smoker, and more oozed onto the floor, mixing with brisket and pork grease. One of our workers was, in effect, ice skating in sneakers, trying to clean up the mess, and trying his best not to fall down—it was that slick. I was lamely scooping beans out of the smoker with a sauté pan, and using mass amounts of terry cloth towels to mop up. All while dinner service was going on.

Jesus, Mary and Joseph.

TEN

....

AND THE HITS JUST KEEP ON COMING

Despite the chaos of the first couple of days, we soldiered on, putting one club foot in front of the other. For most of that summer we were literally packed to the gills. The problem was that we were packed but still making mistakes, many times at the expense of the customers and ultimately us. I was and am utterly astounded by some of the mistakes we made over those next few weeks. A few gems:

In an effort to make a great burger, we pre-seasoned our meat: one teaspoon of Kosher salt per pound of meat. It seasons the meat and makes it juicier. What do you think happens if you put in one *tablespoon* instead? Literally three times the salt. I will tell you: you get a burger that's so salty you have to spit it out. Happened.

We sold about 30 seawater burgers before I found the mistake.

Beef brisket can be hard to make if you're trying to make the best in the country. But for a good eating brisket, even a great one, it is remarkably easy: salt and pepper the brisket, put it fat side up in the smoker, and let it smoke for 12 hours or so. How do you fuck that up? You put them in fat side down. This way, the fat that normally bathes the meat drips uselessly down into the bowels of the smoker, and the remaining meat is dry as dirt and tough as jerky, that's how. This happened too. We lost about 60 servings this way.

Mashed potatoes should be easy, right? I mean, you boil them, drain them, mash with butter, milk, and seasonings, and presto! But if you don't drain them well, and *over salt* the water, you get a very salty vichyssoise. Which ideally should not be served. You guessed it, and yes we did.

One of the things I can honestly say we never screwed up was the coleslaw. But that's kind of like saying that I've never stabbed my eye out while brushing my teeth. I mean shit, it's three ingredients or so and you don't even cook it. But that did not prevent one angry customer from sending me an anonymous letter, postmarked in another city, to tell me if I didn't change the recipe we would go out of business. I wonder if that's why we eventually did?

One of our mistakes that stands out now involves my old nemesis: the aluminum turkey pans. I booked a catering gig at our summer music festival that needed to be delivered to the venue at 5pm, again, coinciding nicely with an already packed restaurant. We had no vehicle to deliver the catering, since our Chevy Suburban was in the shop, so we enlisted Kim's brother and his 1985 Subaru Outback. At 4:45pm he had not arrived, and since the town was swollen with summer visitors and festival goers, making it to the venue on time was going to be a serious problem. He arrived lackadaisically at 4:55pm and we loaded up the Subaru, serving pans in back, stacked on top of each other.

Here are a few things to note: first, you must drive a loaded catering vehicle like you are carrying dynamite, and second, our restaurant sat on a busy highway with extremely short windows in which to pull out. Seething, I sat in the passenger seat, alternating my gaze between my ticking watch and the traffic on the highway. When a gap appeared, Chris floored the old wagon and all of those pans slid backward, since we had not placed towels or anything between them to provide sufficient drag. They rammed into the tailgate, folding up like a deck chair. "Chris! Slow down," I screamed. And he did. He jammed on the brakes and those same pans flew forward, slamming against the back seat, completing the job that the tailgate started. We pulled off onto the shoulder and examined the damage. It was a Jackson Pollock painting. Beans and coleslaw commingled on the carpet. We lost half of what we'd brought. Thankfully, we always brought more than we needed so it ended up OK.

We were not on time, but neither were the guests. For his trouble, Chris had a new shade of carpet and a decidedly different odor that a hundred of those little green gas station deodorant trees couldn't wipe away.

Early on Kim was giddy, since we were well past our revenue projections. But the restaurant operator in me was watching the incrementally slow, consistent sales decline. Gradually, in Sandpoint, the restaurant honeymoon ends and the real work of surviving starts. After Labor Day, business almost literally comes to a halt. We laid off all but a handful of key workers and reduced our hours of operation, as most do in town. Of course this meant I worked more hours to compensate. Herein lies the difficulty of operating a restaurant in a small tourist town: the summer, the most glorious time of the year, requires working crazy hours because you're extremely crowded, and the winter requires working crazy hours because you are short-staffed to accommodate the revenue shortfall. The rest of the year, you worry.

Around spring, when our money started to dry up, we held a board meeting and I decided to stop paying myself a salary. This was not as bad as it seems. I still got to work nights and weekends. Shortly thereafter, I talked to Kim about selling the place. The land had appreciated significantly in the real estate boom and I reasoned that if we sold, we would all at least come out whole and maybe even make some money. She would have none of it; she felt it wouldn't be fair to the investors and we would be quitting only a few months in.

That, and she kept hearing (from people who I am now sure have absolutely no clue from where they speak) that it takes three years to establish a business in Sandpoint.

We ended up raising more cash from one investor, the prince from Los Angeles. This allowed us to limp into the next summer when, we reasoned, we would make enough money to get us through the following winter and spring, like many do around here. The problem was that it wasn't our honeymoon anymore and our numbers never even got close the first summer. We tried everything I could think of: feeding the high school football team for free for PR, adding steaks to the menu since it seemed every other customer clamored for them, and running cute but desperate radio ads featuring our young children.

By fall we were in a pickle. We had no money left, and no viable selling option as the land bubble had burst. Like my mother, I called on the big three, but the big three I invoked were booze, credit cards and antidepressants. As many desperate entrepreneurs do, we applied for, and received, more credit cards than we deserved that we used for cash advances to make payroll, and to pay our vendors. Desperation to keep the doors open also fueled some other efforts that now seem ludicrous:

Since we had a full basement below the former Chinese restaurant that was also at one time a brothel, and since we had a beer and wine license, I decided to use the square footage to open a discount wine store. Never mind that the basement flooded every spring and you needed galoshes to shop there most of the year, and never mind that there was a huge disconnect in driving to the local BBQ restaurant to pick up a bottle of chardonnay. So I used some new credit cards to charge a few thousand dollars in wine inventory, fairly optimistic that this idea would work. We did sell some wine, but the lion's share I think I drank.

I revised the menu about seven times, certain that it was the available choices that were the problem. We added wings. We added fish and chips. And at the behest of an investor's wife, we put in a 70s-era salad bar complete with a soup of the day. Fuck me. A salad bar. I had officially jumped the shark. But I did draw the line at her request for a Panini sandwich press.

We established a high-end catering arm of the company that, while moderately successful, was competing with the handful of other caterers in town for those very few holiday parties and weddings. We bottled our own BBQ sauce, about 20 cases of it, whose sales I was optimistic would take off in a grass roots fashion. It didn't.

But the best, the thing that showed how desperate and delusional I truly was, had to be this: The Duke's Cowboy Grill Bocce Ball Court. That is *not* a typographical error.

Understanding this concept requires patience; admittedly the logic is elusive, and I'm the one whose idea it was. Bocce ball would bring in hordes of people—in North Idaho—who have NEVER heard of it before, let alone grown up playing it on their country estates in Tuscany. Oh, they would come, Ray, they would come in lines of traffic and form leagues. They would appreciate the perfectly leveled, correctly measured, crushed-oyster-shell court. They would chat and play and argue, all the while drinking beer and eating barbecue. But I am not James Earl Jones, and this was not *Field of Dreams*. They didn't come, the court eventually sprouted weeds, and I'm quite certain it caused a lot of giggles and curious blank stares from locals. I'm just happy it was hidden from the highway, it might have caused a wreck.

It's hard to show up at your restaurant every day expecting a crowd and instead getting one or two tables of folks who used ranch dressing like a beverage. So I drank. Often, a lot. Combined with the antidepressants that I got from my doctor at my wife's request, it dulled the pain. It also dulled my reflexes to the point that one evening I dumped an entire tray of beers on an unsuspecting table of early bird seniors. But then again, that might be the most fun they'd had in a while.

Slowly, we ran out of money, available credit, and any remnants of our sanity. We closed the weeping sore that was our restaurant about two weeks after the last menu revision, complete with new graphic design, and about three weeks after our very large chili cook-off designed to show the place off to anyone who had not been there.

Now, years later, people tell me quite often how much they loved the restaurant and they are sorry it's closed. After thinking, "Where the hell were you when it was open?" I thank them. Friends ask me now if it makes me sad. No. Not exactly. Deliriously happy, more like. No more dealing with employees who have no branches in their family tree. No more finding whole prime ribs forgotten in the now-cold holding cabinet all night. No more old men leaving medieval movements in the men's restroom and then waddling out to their Plymouth. No more being telephoned while enjoying a movie with my family by an investors' wife saying that the restaurant was too cold—in the dead of winter. And no more standing at a cash register at noon on a Friday with a thousand-yard stare hoping for one car to pull into the parking lot. Just one. Of the experience, I sometimes think of the Chinese proverb that "the journey is the reward," and conclude that Helen Keller must have translated that one.

ELEVEN

··

THE HOUSE

The plumber must have just left. I know this because there is a handwritten bill sitting on our overpriced teak love seat we bought years ago from the now-defunct Smith and Hawken stores, and now gathers dust and socks in our entryway. Here is another beautiful yet hard to get used to fact of small town life: once you become known to a service company—and this takes as much as one visit—they will happily send you the bill after the fact, and can be trusted to enter your premises and do their work while you are not home. So it is that Joe the Plumber (not making that up) came and snaked our main sewer line that clogs quarterly. The line itself runs to the street and is made of terra cotta pipe (think Etruscans) and therefore can't take too much of this-century toilet paper. We should have the whole thing torn up and redone. Whatever.

My wife and I agree quite happily that we are not meant to be homeowners. We are meant to be renters. Or maybe condominium owners with a maintenance fee and upkeep. Actually, that's not true either. Ideally, we should live in a hotel.

To be a good homeowner, you need to be able to fix things. You need to be able to, or have the desire to, learn how to garden, even if the growing season is woefully short. You need to like, and have some interest in, home decorating. And you need to be diligent enough to recognize when things need upkeep, when decks need refinishing or stain, that exterminators need to be called at the beginning of seasons, or that the furnace guy needs to be called in the fall to get ready for winter. In other words, you need to be sort of on the ball. My inabilities in these areas are even more glaring in rural Idaho. Most people in the Idaho Panhandle, whether they are the "The Rapture is Nigh" types or not, are self-sufficient. They know how to do things. Women and men.

If you have too many negatives on one side of the DIY equation, you need to be able to balance the other side with money. Then, even if you're as delusional as Charlie Manson, you can call in the cavalry to help. We have neither. Neither the appropriate skills or diligence, nor the cash. But here's the sad part: we have just enough common sense to know this, and just enough awareness to realize how pathetic we are. So, like the people we are, we balance long periods of denial, short periods of angst, and even shorter periods of actual home repair inspired by HGTV, and fortified by numerous trips to Home Depot. (I really don't think I've ever fixed anything—*anything*—with one trip to the hardware store. And "fix" is a relative term; I am including changing light bulbs.)

So, knowing this, and we knew this relatively early on in our marriage, do you think that prevented us from buying a large, rambling, 100-year-old fixer upper in Sandpoint, Idaho? It most certainly did not. If you remember, we moved our entire family to Austin, Texas because we thoroughly enjoyed our stays at the Four Seasons Hotel there. We assumed when we moved to Austin that The Four Seasons lifestyle would somehow be ours. We would enjoy commanding views of Town Lake, and enjoy freshly squeezed margaritas. What we got was a cookie-cutter home 10 miles outside of Austin proper, and a yard with no trees that, in the baking summer sun, resembled Tranquility Base on the moon. Our housing choices are not beyond reproach.

We first encountered our house when Kim's former boss invited us over for dinner. We had driven by the house before and admired it, despite the siding that needed replacing during the Johnson administration. When we saw the inside, it was love at first sight. The old hulk was built around 1907. I think the style is Queen Anne, but I only know that because someone told me. I really have no idea. It has been a residence, a boarding house, a nursing home and a motel. There are millions of old pipes that zigzag inside and out. The basement pipes alone would take years to sort out. My father-in-law once asked me where our main water turn off was. I looked at him like he was from the future. I didn't know what a main turn off was, let alone where ours was among the spaghetti of pipes. At one time there were six electric meters out back; in fact, the former owner used to get six electric bills. Parts of the interior have been redone, mainly to bring some of the amenities into this century, and some were redone to make so many of the former small, pocketed rooms into livable space. But much of the funky oldness remains. There are huge mahogany beams and molding in every downstairs room, with lathe and plaster walls. Much of the maple flooring is reclaimed basketball gym flooring from the old high school. This floor loses about three inches in elevation from one end of the foundation to the other, so you can start your favorite Hot Wheels race car at one end and watch it rocket to the other without assistance. The kids loved that when they were tots.

The house sits in South Sandpoint, four blocks from our local marina, and five or six blocks in the other direction to a swimming pier. The elementary school, our high school, our local burger and ice cream joint, and most importantly Starbucks, are all within walking distance. Kim walks to work in the morning as it is *faster* than taking the car and parking it. We walk to the 4th of July parade and can easily stumble home from any late night outing. One of the local bars—that we have never been to out of fear—is so close we hear some of the patrons in drunken conversations at 2am, assisted by the excellent acoustic properties of the hundred-year-old maples that dot the neighborhood and surround our house. To be even more precise, our house sits squarely in a section of Sandpoint known as Kellyville. This is because a few years ago, Kim's parents, *The Kellys*, decided to abandon their lakefront house on one of the prettiest bays of Lake Pend Oreille and build a house about 30 feet from ours. Of course I have not measured this; some things you just *know*. They are of the "good home-owner" ilk. They do strange things like maintenance before things break, garden, and decorate. The fact that their brand new home is state-of-art and shouldn't require any maintenance yet makes the contrast from our home even more glaring. Figuratively, too, I live in Kellyville. Of course any son-in-law lives in his own version of this town, population: 1.

We never really entertained the idea of living in this old house, but when my wife's former boss decided to move—had to move, really, as he had a new job in Montana—he offered us the place at a good deal. The sentimental old sap thought our kids *needed* an old house like this. He *wanted* us to live there. Either that, or he saw some chumps standing right there in front of him who would not ask any questions remotely linked to the cost of ownership. For us it was serendipity!

But big decisions, you know the ones, marriage, kids, homes, should be made with both the heart and the head. It's like *those* girls in high school: they're hot and they're fun to fantasize about, but that does not mean you should get into a long-term relationship with them.

Yes. We bought the place. Again. Four Seasons. Austin.

Our house has beautiful sidewalks that wrap around the entire corner lot. These same sidewalks require snow blowing the whole winter, unless you're one of those assholes who doesn't blow his sidewalks, and although I may become one, I am not that guy . . . yet. These same sidewalks require upkeep. It seems the Sandpoint city code operates in an alternative realm where normal logic does not apply, at least my logic. To wit: the city owns the sidewalks, which sit on our property, but we as homeowners are required to keep them up and replace them when necessary. This was truly excellent news, since the aforementioned old growth trees refused to stop growing, despite my hollow chainsaw threats. Their roots tore through the sidewalks like butter, and so we spent $8,000 to replace them.

We have a very nice-sized yard with an annoying feature: it requires mowing. This can be an adventure since the yard that looks relatively flat is actually an optical illusion. The roots from the aforementioned trees (this will become a theme) have created bumps and divots throughout the yard. The mower shucks and jives the whole time, and at best the result is a bad haircut. It also requires fertilizer, more than one bag but not quite two. A bonus. I assumed, erroneously, that one can leave the leftovers in the spreader until the next time to fertilize. It's possible, once you chisel the newly formed fertilizer mass back into little bits.

Back to the trees. I would have killed for them when we lived in Texas, to provide at least a bit of shade. There are six. Most are old maples. One is a horse chestnut that I just call a cocksucker. Oh, sure, it gives nice shade in the summer, but it is ugly as hell, and once a year, true to its name, sheds chestnuts—hundreds of them. They are not rakeable, they are too heavy. They can't be mowed, since they split into chunks and just lie there. Even the squirrels are sensible enough not to eat them. So what do you do? I'm not sure, but I think you are supposed to pick them up by hand. One year I had a light bulb moment: pay the kids to pick them up. At that time they were small, and therefore dumb. Or gullible. It's just semantics. So I gathered the little dimwits around and without thinking, offered them 10 cents for every chestnut they gathered. When they were done, the lawn and leaf bag would not hold them, it tore from the weight. I lost count at 400 chestnuts. That pencils out to $40. Now to a kid, *four bucks* is Bill Gates money. Forty bucks is beyond the imagination. People who hear this story, people with at least a tablespoon of grey matter in their heads, look at me like the moron I am. But I did pay up. I may call my kids dimwits, and used to make them run around the house to tire them out, but I pay up on my deals.

It's not just that chestnut tree, though. The maples aren't much better. Those bastards throw off truckloads of leaves, every fall. When the kids were wee, the leaf piles were easily taller than they were. They had great fun diving into them off of our deck until, of course, they dove into the occasional piece of dog shit. Thankfully all we have to do is rake the piles to the curb for the city to pick up some time in November. Even this is a pain in the ass. If we're lucky, it will rain incessantly during the season, turning those feather light leaves into rake-breaking piles of concrete. If we're really lucky? Snow. Then we can't get them to the curb by the time the city picks them up, so nature gives us Christmas three times: once in the fall, once again in the winter, and then again in the spring. Each year I fantasize about carrying out my chainsaw threat, but that would expose our house's crumbling siding to the world, as well as incur the wrath of the "tree-lady" who lives a few blocks over. For the landscaping, or rather gardening, it both helps and hurts that Kim's mother is a certified master gardener. She helps us, but just enough. She wouldn't dare become an enabler. It is for our own good, and for that we are grateful.

Eventually, we thought when we bought the place, we would make gradual improvements and renovations. Our report card here is as spotty as mine from college, but we have made some improvements. It's just there's so damn much to be done, compounded by our annoying apathy. In these old places, built before the time of pads and pods and charging stations, they only needed one electrical outlet per room, most likely for the console radio. And in most rooms, that is what we have. So my son Jackson's room has multiple extension cords snaking around to power fans and iPods. What should have been at the top of any sensible person's home improvement list is window replacement. Upstairs we have done this, except for our eldest son's room, because we figured he was off to college anyway. But downstairs, most windows are of the ancient wavy glass variety. The bad thing about this is heat loss. We heat the entire neighborhood. I have no doubt that our home's infrared heat signature is visible from space. I am not exaggerating here: the power company sends us regular notifications that they fear we might have a gas leak due to our massive consumption. Of course they also send us notifications that they think we have a water leak as well. We suspect it has something to do with the six or so laundry loads a week, and the fact that our youngest likes to unwind from his grueling 10-hour sleep with a 15-minute hot shower. Laundry itself is an infinite loop. There is never a time that the washer or dryer is not full. Unfolded clothes sit in laundry baskets on the floor in our master bedroom, since the laundry machines reside in our master closet. The clean clothes make it at least that far, never truly in danger of being folded and put away. Every morning, boys parade into our bedroom to enter the sock and underwear lottery. On more than one occasion I have put on the wrong underwear, that of a male 100 pounds lighter than me, only to have the underwear come full stop at my thighs, at which point I topple over. Kim occasionally deigns to fold our clothes when the inspiration appears from the ether. But she will not put those clothes away. It is somehow beneath her, and I am not brave enough to question her logic.

We had an excuse for our malaise early on, since we had a new restaurant and a brain-dead puppy to contend with. At that time, we just tried to keep up. We changed not a thing. It was our boys versus the house, and the boys won. An antique chandelier exploded, seemingly without cause. The tennis ball that rolled across the floor absolutely could not have been the culprit, since apparently no one threw it. An antique ceiling fan that one of our local historians said was dated from about 1937 or so mysteriously lost three of four blades. Our bedroom window shattered from an errant throw of a Ping-Pong paddle. As time passed, we started to run out of excuses, and still we did nothing. At one time I was curious how all of those people on home makeover shows could actually not see the squalor they were exposing to the world on cable TV. Now I understand.

It's not all active destruction, though: things sometimes wear out, or require accessories to make them livable. For these, I have, over time, come up with a solution. It is a toolkit of binder clips, duct tape, a butter knife, aluminum foil, and most importantly: a blind eye and a basement.

Binder clips come in handy should you need to attach towels or sheets to window molding to block out annoying sunlight. A butter knife is essential in lieu of a screwdriver for fixing the screen door handle and the odd kitchen cabinet that pops off. Duct tape? Obvious: it holds up the louvers on our portable air conditioner, covers the divot that came from a wrestling match in the lone sheetrock wall, and seals the burst water pipe in the garage. (It seems you need to turn off outdoor water in the winter.) Aluminum foil, so handy in the kitchen, came to the rescue when the top of one of the antique outdoor lamps that sit atop two concrete pillars at the entrance to our house disappeared. A vandal, or more likely a drunk on the way home from a downtown bar, removed it as a souvenir. When an Internet search to replace it proved worthless, since it is an antique, I found a piece of a wine box that I probably used for the ill-advised Halloween tombstones and cut it into roughly the same shape as the base to the lamp top. This I covered with aluminum foil in order to waterproof it. I forced it into the fixture and presto! All fixed.

But the silver bullet is the blind eye. Or denial. Take your pick. We just adapt around the broken item.

When the "his" of the "his and hers" pedestal sink started leaking behind the porcelain pedestal, I sprang into action. Outfitted with my trusty LL Bean coal miner headlamp, I quickly deduced that yes, it was indeed leaking. But I mistakenly thought that it was leaking from the drain fixture, since that little bugger had some give in it where it met the porcelain of the sink. This would be child's play. Armed with a tube of caulk and ham hands, I slathered caulk on the drain so it looked like somebody did it while wearing welding goggles. I went to test it and guess what? Yes, it still leaked. So I put on my uniform and assessed it again. It was leaking from behind, inside the pedestal. I put on a latex glove, slathered the caulk on the glove, and set about to effectively finger paint the leak—that I could not see—closed. There was a very small chance this would succeed, and it did not. The solution: a blind eye. We have not used that sink since. It has been six years and counting. Now it holds odds and ends like razors and floss. The antique claw foot bathtub in our master bath, fully plumbed but lacking fixtures, holds swimsuits, beach towels, and the intake hose for that portable air conditioner unit that we break out in the summer.

When our microwave that sits atop the built-in oven died a few years back, we simply repurposed it to hold bags of chips. The dead kitchen stereo speakers are fancy design elements. Broken fence slats enable us a clearer view of Kim's parents' house. The entry way may contain generations of tennis shoes, but we don't see them. The final solution, when all else fails, is to throw the offending item, if it is not attached to the structure, into the basement and slam the door. The basement itself is fantastically creepy. It was a natural spot to hide Christmas presents, since the kids wouldn't go anywhere near it. The dog doesn't even like it down there, choosing instead to wait at the top of the stairs and whine. This prompted Joe the plumber, himself a ghost hunter, to conclude that the basement was indeed haunted. If it is, I sure wish the ghosts could tidy it up a bit.

TWELVE

....

BRISKET AND ME

Christ, what a dog.

Like many men, once I had kids and a family I thought we should then have a dog. A big ol' dog. Slobber? Who cares. Shedding? Who cares. Barking in the middle of the night? Wait a second.

When our boys were wee and we were all together as a family, people often made the inevitable "my you have your hands full!" comment. I would then reach into my grab bag of tired material and explain that having three boys instead of two was simply a shift from man-to-man defense to zone defense. This was one of my better lines, actually, that I ripped off, allowing me to show off my sports creds and my sense of humor in one fell swoop. However, when someone used to ask what it was like to have three boys, each two years apart, I would jokingly say, "Get a dog, it's easier, and you can beat it." Uncomfortable silence ensued.

Of course I was joking about the beating part. Sort of. If the truth were told, a dog is every bit as hard as a small child. Worse, actually. I think I read somewhere that a dog has the IQ of a two-year-old. Well, depending on the breed, I would argue that a dog actually has the IQ of a mentally retarded two-year-old. My dog, at least. The breed and dog in question? A 120-pound black lab. *Stupidus eateverythingus.*

He would be on our Christmas cards wearing goofy reindeer antlers. He would accompany me on runs and, of course, swim with us in the lake and happily retrieve balls from the water. He would ride in the car with his big stupid dog head hanging out the window, tongue lolling, in a state of bliss. I wanted a dog because I had dogs growing up, but more than that I wanted a dog for the kids. "Boys need dogs," an ex-friend once told me. Boys also need to masturbate, but my wife and I don't actively promote that idea.

The one big delusion I was under, or perhaps denial is a better word, is that this would be a family dog. Kim has long made it clear that she doesn't really like dogs. Despite having grown up with dogs, she didn't like them. She hated her after school chore: walking Abba, her black Labrador retriever that I met when we first started dating. Abba was a loveable 400 pounder, as wide as she was tall, that would eat anything off the floor— from lime peels to bottle caps. But evidently Abba, named after the Swedish rock group, scarred her for life. I thought a cute little puppy would change that.

Change a 40-year-old woman. Yes, you read that right, and yes, I did think it.

Once.

But at least, *at least*, the kids would love the dog. They would happily walk it and play with it. No, they wouldn't like scooping its poop, but out of their sheer love for the dog, and my gentle prodding, they would do so. Spoiler alert: due to a combination of factors, among them laziness on the part of our kids, a heart of ice on the part of my wife, and the doggy instinctive trait of loyalty to the alpha male Labradors possess that borders on the insane, this dog is all mine.

Let's start at the beginning. He was, once, a small, adorable puppy that melts your heart as only puppies can, but especially small Labradors with their oversized paws predicting how massive they will be. I decided to name him Brisket, because at the time we had *just* opened Duke's Cowboy Grill, and wouldn't that be oh so cute to have a dog named Brisket? Pretty damn cute, but did I consider that if the restaurant were to crater (yes) he would be a constant reminder of my failures? No, I did not. And if that seems unusual, please remember that we bought a brand new puppy the week we opened a new restaurant.

Stanford just called. They want my diploma back.

Thankfully, "Brisket" is only on his driver's license. We have come to call him Pooper, in part because his shits are truly epic, and often times he will shit multiple times. This happens mostly when I am walking him past a house with a picture window, when he has already shat once, and I have therefore used up my flimsy Wal-Mart poop bag. Part of this multi-shit performance, I believe, goes back to the manic nature he has of *not letting me out of his SIGHT*. If I start to get ahead of him while he is in the act, he dutifully pinches off and resumes the walk only to strike again, sometimes blocks away. Fun fact: the most shits he has taken on a half-hour walk is four. I spell out "four" not only because Strunk and White told me to spell out numbers below 10, but because it emphasizes the sheer quantity there: f-o-u-r. Another fun fact: he once did his business in the middle of the street while I was biking him to the lake for a swim. When duty called, he became a rock of black granite, squatting in the middle of the street. I hit the brakes. Unfortunately, the brakes on Kim's shitty street cruiser had been disengaged from a tire change a few weeks prior. Madly I tried the Fred Flintstone method of stopping. No. As I looked back, hoping he was done, all I saw was that universal expression for man and beast when trying to accomplish their business. I shot over the handlebars into the street, in front of our local steakhouse, and then I had to limp back to scoop up the pile from the hot asphalt. That was a good day.

Yes, this dog is mine. All in. I can't even get the kids to play with the damn thing anymore. Whose kids don't want to play with a dog? Mine, that's whose. Of course, I will say that it's not entirely their fault. Brisket has a way of ruining activities the way a boorish drunk does a party.

Brisket has two obsessions, the first are his balls. Not those of course. He is a eunuch and has never known the joys of having his own pair. He obsesses over balls of the bouncy variety. I am fully aware that many dogs enjoy a good ball. I am also fully aware that the mere fact any breed with the word "retriever" in it would imply a canine that liked to go and get things and bring them back. However, to assume that these two qualifiers would imply a level of behavior that could somehow be construed as normal would be wrong. Very, very wrong.

This dog obsesses about balls the way I do about, well, sex. If you introduce a ball into his environment, he simply must possess it like Lenny and his rabbits. And like Lenny, he eventually kills his little friends. It is simply too much of a good thing. He chews them to death. He is a connoisseur of balls. His favorite is the racquetball, followed closely by the tennis ball. He has a really annoying habit of making love to them in his mouth, which makes a thoroughly disgusting sound. More annoying, though, is that he drops them at your feet repeatedly until you break down and throw it or kick it. If you throw the ball once, you have to throw it a million fucking times. He simply does not tire out. And if he does tire, he then *will not* drop his ball for you to throw it. He simply hangs on to what is now a barely recognizable sphere encased in about a half-inch of dog slobber. When we take long walks, this amount of dog foam reaches a critical mass of sorts. He then shakes his head to readjust the ball's position, and that jettisons this slobber-foam anywhere in a five-foot radius. Half the time it shoots right back onto his coat, giving him his own version of racing stripes.

The fact that he wouldn't drop his neon yellow Penn ATP used to drive my kids crazy, because I used to put limits on how many times they needed to throw the ball for the dog as a daily chore. This rule came about because when I simply asked the boys to walk him, it became painfully obvious, as it would to any parent, how far they would go: one block. One block to a young lab is a joke. So, there was a manager-induced pitch count. And thus, no drop = no get to come inside. The little dears had to wait him out until he chose to drop his ball. And a dog in a fur coat in the snow can wait a long time.

Inevitably, we must take the ball away. But it is not enough to simply take away his ball, that would be too easy. If the ball is within his purview, and keep in mind he is about 5'2" stretched out, so his purview is pretty damn large, he moans. I mean, like a doggy dirge. Thanks again to his infinitesimally small brain, however, out of sight, way out of mind.

You would think that one of his obsessions would be eating, as any Labrador retriever's owner will tell you. Not this dog. Leave it to me, with my love of food and a restaurant background, to have gotten a canine version of a foodie. Sometimes he skips meals because he thinks he is missing out on something, like a walk, or some other version of exercise. On other days, he boycotts his food because it is not to his liking. I have started to do what other friends have done and I swore never to do: I put something extra in his food. I do not make him eggs as, a friend of mine does. I cook for my own animals, but not of the dog variety. But I do sprinkle a bit of parmesan cheese on his food. Ugh. Other days, though, he skips his food because I swear he forgets it's there.

The worst part about the dog? It's not his massive shits, nor the bales of fur that he distributes in and all over our house when he sheds, which is all year long. (I find his fur on the lips of bottles of cooking oil that I have screwed shut. How is this possible? He's the Harry Houdini of shedding.) It's not his barking, or his pterodactyl tail that knocks over wine glasses. No, it is his main obsession: me. He stalks me. I've said that he has the alpha male devotion thing in spades, but it is more than that. He not only wants to be where I am, or see me at all times, he is also afraid of my leaving him, at any time. I might take a trip to Wal-Mart, and that would mean missing a car ride. So, he stalks me. If I move with anything close to alacrity, he jumps. Getting up from my desk! Going to the sink! Peeing! Crossing my legs! It is truly maddening. It shows how small, repeated movements have the power to drive you crazy. I wonder what kind of story Poe could have written about this one-eyed wonder. That fixed stare. *The Black Cat* becomes *The Black Dog*. It gives me shivers.

And beware lest you encourage him. You will have his blockhead in your lap and his incessantly wagging tail knocking over anything in reach, begging—no, willing—you to get up and get that hidden tennis ball and throw it for him. This is not cute. This is finely-honed manipulation. But it still inspires a question: how does a good, occasionally fun, and almost always fulfilling thing become something you don't want to encourage? I would imagine paying attention to our dog is not unlike a woman (my wife) paying attention to a man (me). It all leads somewhere you don't want to go. I know if I pet my dog, he will get excited, pick up his big black paws and start pawing me, and inevitably want me to play. Same thing for my wife. Attention leads to, at first, good-natured petting that inevitably leads to the ball thing, in some form or other.

However, I am not the only living thing Brisket stalks. Woe to you if you are a flying insect in the spring and summer. Then, his focus turns to you. Death might come as he corners you against a windowpane and dispatches you down his gullet, leaving a six-inch smear of slobber on the glass. We stopped cleaning our windows in the warmer months years ago. Fly season means hazy windows. He springs to the attack when he hears the telltale buzzing, or he hears the cabinet open where we keep the fly swatter. Sometimes I assist in the slaughter. It is as close he and I will ever get to hunting together; instead of ducks, we hunt flies. Brisket is not limited to just flies, although they are his snack of choice. No, he goes after yellow jackets and bald-faced hornets with equal gusto. For these, he has worked out a system: he uses the chomp and release method of eating them that looks a lot like me trying to eat pizza that is too hot. Pleasure and pain. After a few weeks of being stung in the mouth and on the tongue, though, he eventually decides to allow me to kill anything with venom. As many flies as he has maimed, killed, and swallowed alive, he is never satisfied. It appears he is looking for that one fly, the trophy fly, his white whale. And as such, his quest continues.

Our hero was not born a cyclops, it was earned. It came at the claws of our cat, who is as mean as he is lovable. And as fat. He eats like Kobiyashi. We originally found him abandoned in the shed behind the restaurant during its renovation. We cleverly named him Smokey for his grey fur, and the BBQ restaurant tie-in. We are nothing if not consistent. When he is in the mood to love, he loves, otherwise he is an assassin. His pastime is removing birds as well as bats from their flight paths. Occasionally, he even scores a hummingbird, which drives our bird-loving neighbor crazy. I do not tell her that I think it's quite the ninja move, but inside I am swelling with pride. If birds are not readily available, he likes to hunt our youngest son, or at least he used to when Sam was small. The miniature tiger would lie in wait on the stairs, blending into the carpeting. Once the attack was launched, he would then haul his balls to our room and wait out the aftermath under the bed. Our other two sons took pleasure in this, reminding Sam that he was the cat's "bitch."

The cat barely tolerates the dog, his disdain apparent on his little cat face. They never really bonded. My wife, who has her hate-hate relationship with our dog, likes to say this is because the dog is just like me: he eats without chewing his food, is a pain in the ass until he gets some exercise, and likes to hump anything, anytime. I have no idea why she brings this up, nor how this has anything to do with how Smokey feels about the dog. Nevertheless, I respond by telling her that our cat is just like her: aloof, only willing to dole out affection when he damn well feels like it, and is happy to lie on the couch all day. We are at an impasse. Other than his just existing, one reason Smokey hates Brisket is because the dog loves chasing him. It is his crack pipe. The cat does not realize that the dog would do him no harm should he be successful. No. This is just like when he raced out on our half-frozen lake to chase geese during the winter. Were they to stop, and they did, the dog would turn and look at me with a half-crazed expression that said, "Now what do I do, Dad?" The fun is in the chasing.

But back to his eyeball. On the day in question, all the dog did was lay his massive square head on the bed where Smoky was lounging with our eldest. A flick of a razor sharp paw and the deed was done. Of course it wasn't that fast, eyeballs just don't fall out. That would be too easy. This would require a trip to the local vet and expensive antibiotics. They thought he was better. He was back to his old self, and then he got worse. This misdiagnosis earned us a trip to Spokane, 90 minutes each way, to visit a doggy eye specialist. Apparently there is such a thing. And he was fabulous, but he could not save the eye. The doctor needed to vacuum that little sucker out. Despite the fact that the patient had four legs, this was not cheap. Rather, it cost a shit ton. Kim, when she heard, asked how much "the shot" would have cost.

That shot.

For future reference, that shot is less than a hundred bucks. I never even almost considered it. Happily for the patient, he doesn't miss the eyeball. Having only one eye has really presented few problems for him, aside from the occasional crack of his head on a table leg when he doesn't know it's there. We advise guests as callous as we that it's OK to laugh; it's quite funny in a slapstick sort of way. Oh, and he has a devil of a time finding the flight of his favorite tennis ball if it has been thrown off-line, or if it's too covered in slobber to be less than bright yellow. Both happen A LOT. Kim likes to ask the dog where his eyeball is. And the best part? The dog only hears the word "ball," and eagerly wags his tail. Somewhere along the way, that sweet co-ed I married has morphed into a monster.

One year later, behold, another health scare for our darling. He seemed to have picked up *Giardia* somewhere in the standing water along our town's bike path. Or so we thought. Once expensive antibiotics failed to cure him, we tried a barium-expensive-X-ray-expensive doctor's visit. Jackpot. We found it. Guess what it was. Did you guess that he swallowed a handball? Could you have guessed that if you had 100 tries? He did, and there's no way to pass it. If I had known how much that procedure was going to cost, I would have KYed my arm and gone after it myself. After a brief doggy C-section, out it came, swollen to the size of a tennis ball. He regained his health and put back on the 15 or so pounds he lost by vomiting all over the house, in pretty short order.

As of the latest ailment (a mysterious intestinal infection that, of course, could not be diagnosed with the expensive digital X-rays we had done, but rather had to be treated with an expensive overnight vet stay and expensive antibiotics that cost more than $500) our little boy, nay middle-aged man, has cost us over $3500.

Friends, dog lovers to be sure, advise me that, "Duke, that really only works out to be about $1.50 per day for the dog." Depending on how close friends they are, I might just then advise *them* to go fuck themselves.

Should anyone consider purchasing a Labrador retriever, especially the high-energy American lab, I have put together a questionnaire as a public health service. The answers to the self-guided questions are simply yes or no. A dog like this demands it:

- I want a dog that takes extraordinarily large craps. Craps like a bear.
- I want a dog that sheds like a motherfucker, winter or summer, makes no difference.

- I want a dog with a brain that is not fully formed. Fully formed perhaps for a single-celled amoeba, but for a mammal, no.
- I want a dog that is stubborn and damned near bulletproof, to make training more of a challenge: "Sit? What sit? I want to chase squirrels. Dog whisperer? Go fuck yourself. Hit me, I can't feel it."
- I want a dog so large I can't carry it. With a tail so strong it can knock over full wine bottles.
- I want a dog that sticks to me like glue. Going in the crapper? I'll come too.

If you answered yes to a majority of these, congratulations! You are as brain-dead as the dog you are about to spend the next dozen years with.

THIRTEEN

THE SELKIRK BAKERY

At some point in the Sandpoint odyssey, I became a baker. No, not a full-fledged baker; that can take years learning the nuance of breads, or the intricacies of decorating cakes. I was more of a Bubbles the Chimp-type baker.

Not long after we closed Duke's Cowboy Grill, I started looking for work and had about as much success as I'd had the previous 10 years when trying to find work outside of the food service arena. Oh, there was work, but it certainly wasn't a living wage. So, like any able-bodied man, I turned to the same place we turn to for porn or sports updates: the Internet. I looked at it this way: I have developed a bit of knowledge about food and restaurant operations, and wanted to see if I could leverage it without the shitload of overhead that comes with a brick and mortar business. I stumbled on a legitimate company that teaches folks how to build websites that, if you supply the elbow grease, the knowledge, and the passion, would succeed in search engine rankings. If you succeeded in rankings, the idea goes, you could make money selling ad space or make a commission sending others to sites like Amazon. That's the idea, anyway. Of course there are people who make money this way, but they are the equivalent of Internet billionaires: people who are not you. In the end, I started a website about what else? True BBQ.

One Friday afternoon, while I was in the research phase of the website that consisted of picking page topics and deciding on the site architecture, Kim came home early. Our boys were watching some brain dead pre-teen comedy that has jokes that don't resemble humor in any form, but have laugh tracks that preach otherwise. Drake and Josh. I fantasized about putting a contract out on those two actors. Since Kim rarely came home early, it felt like a holiday. She came into my office and mouthed some words to me. Her words were:

I. WAS. FIRED. TODAY.

My *single word* was:

FUCK!

I have known my wife for almost 30 years. Other than tearing up at movies, which happens all the time, I have seen her cry twice. The first was when our piece of shit Hyundai Excel (the Korean Pinto) was broken into and Kim's leather auditor's briefcase was stolen. The second time was that night she came home to tell me she was fired from the bank. I mean, she wailed like one of those women from a faraway country on CNN. Feeling utterly powerless, I resorted to what men do best and I got her hammered on vodka.

Like the girl I knew, the crying lasted just that night. The next day she started trying to find work. We decided, much like the Clintons, to get our version of the story out first, except our story was not fiction. We told people frankly that she was fired. In a small town they will find out anyway. And as a life lesson, when you're honest, people accept it and commiserate. The people who knew the situation had already realized that she was a scapegoat for some real estate loans that went south. Loans that an *entire committee* approved. And let's be serious, we needed to tell the truth: nobody would believe the usual line that she just wanted to spend more time with her family. One look at our family would tell you that. For a while then, we were both home together, she working the networking circuit, and I, my new website. Working on building my new goldmine website, I learned a lot. I dreamed a lot. My wife thought I was a moron. One day, in between making calls to colleagues and friends about any open positions, Kim asked me what *my plans were* for getting a job.

And I made a mistake. I told her the truth.

I explained as if to a child that I was going to make enough money to support our family essentially blogging about meat. The look she gave me resembles the look our cat gives a bird. How could I be serious? Was I drunk? Was I taking too much back pain medicine? The arguments started steadily after that, largely about money woes and my apparent disregard for said woes, and that I had my head lodged securely up my asshole. Our marriage to that point had been extremely easy. We had been, and are, lucky. I cannot speak for her, but I married my best friend, who coincidentally I liked to jump. So I never understood friends who complained about how difficult marriage is, and all the compromising that goes with it. We never had any real issues and saw eye-to-eye on most things. But after three or four fights about money, Kim suggested that we needed to see a marriage therapist. I wanted to tell her to go fuck herself, but that might have reinforced her position, and I like to be right.

So we went. The details aren't really important, except to say we went a grand total of two times and I was, by all accounts, proven to be the winner. I know, I know. There's no "winner" in these things. But, I was the winner. Sometimes you need to spend a few hundred bucks for your wife to hear that you *are* taking her seriously, that you *aren't* delusional, and that you *both* value greatly what you have. The therapist also backed up my claim that well-paying jobs, other than for professional types, were exceedingly scarce in Sandpoint, and that her expectations were a tad high. I say it again because it is a rare phenomenon: I won.

Despite my pyrrhic victory, the truth was, I still needed a job that came with a paycheck every two weeks. Perusing the classified ads in our newspaper I came upon

an ad for a morning baker. Whoever codified the job de-
scription "morning baker" was playing fast and loose
with the meaning. Morning bakers start their work so
early they are essentially vampires. Kim did cartwheels;
it was not enough money, but it was a start. She was also
ecstatic—we both were—because the president of the
other bank in town, her former bank's archrival, had interviewed her the week prior. He was creating a new initiative that required a person to oversee and manage,
and would she consider taking the job? Mrs. Magoo,
your girder has arrived.

I interviewed with one of the bakery owners who,
with her graying hippie-chick hair and reading glasses
suspended by a chain, looked like a librarian. This particular co-owners' name was Monique, and she was the
person primarily responsible for decorating wedding
cakes and expediting the cookies and dessert bars.
Knowing this town, the simple fact that I could fill out
an entire generic employment application without skipping sections that were either too difficult, or required
three dreaded references, gave me a leg up on the competition. Also, I was dimwitted enough to be willing to
get up at 4am every day for work. But Monique (I would
call her Mo) and I hit it off, we had the California Bay
Area in common, and she was a real sweetheart, quick to
laugh and passionate about her craft. It turns out she
and her husband were both retired postal workers from
Santa Cruz, California. She went to school in Santa Cruz
in cake decorating, and for some strange reason wanted

to subject herself in her retirement to the demands of not only running a business, but also dealing with brides-to-be. There is not enough money on the planet, nor wine in the fridge, for me to deal with anxious brides-to-be.

She was naturally demanding about how the product looked, and how it tasted, but there was more to it than that. She became almost maniacal when something went wrong. I did not understand why until I met the other owner, her partner. Evidently they'd both worked at the same bakery in Santa Cruz, California, although during different time periods. Mo's partner was a gal named Margot. She is a petite spark plug (attitude, not build) of a woman. She is an avid skier, biker, and former rower, with greying hair cut short and held tightly while at work under a multi-colored baker's cap. She is an accomplished musician and wicked smart. In fact, she and her husband form part of a great local blues band. But to meet her, she can be a tad prickly. And when she is low on blood sugar, which is normally the state she arrives at the bakery, or when she first meets you, she can be a raging bitch. She is also an introvert in the way that Stephen Hawking is a scientist and the Pope is a priest. Introversion bordering on social autism. She makes it clear that she prefers kids to adults, and dogs to people. But the truth be told, she is a blast to have a conversation with. (In the span of one short afternoon, she fluently took me through the history of music, from Mozart and the baroque period through jazz and bebop all the while mixing and weighing dough.) I was fortunate in our relationship in that, since I was a former restaurant owner, I knew where her motivations and stroke-inducing frustrations came from. She wanted things to be perfect and it was normally some uncaring or stupid asshole that fucked things up. And when this happened, well ... no wonder Mo looked like she'd seen a ghost when something went wrong.

The Selkirk Bakery is housed in a hundred-year-old house that, like most buildings in Sandpoint, had been added onto at some point by someone who had no real building experience, and most likely couldn't afford a contractor. The building had gone through many previous owners and business types, and before those it was a residence, back in the days of big timber and waistcoats. I think the last business had been a vegetarian restaurant—a business that's a challenge in California, but in North Idaho? Please. But it is truly a charming building, an old Victorian house very high on the funk-meter. Now, with Mo and Margot running it, it was clean, brightly painted and full of secondhand, barely functioning equipment except for the few precious pieces they'd purchased new. The new pieces of equipment consisted of a genuine Italian-made espresso machine and reach-in refrigerators. All of their other equipment were pieces of shit. Really. But this is to their credit: purchasing kitchen equipment new is expensive and it depreciates faster than a timeshare in Florida. Also, any restaurant, as I thought I knew but relearned the hard way, is only as successful as its investment, whether in FF and Es (furniture, fixtures and equipment) or real estate. A lesson that cost me $550k to learn.

Among the pieces of shit was a free-standing convection oven that had only one temperature: the one that was Sharpied on the dial. Of course it had more than one temperature, but the Sharpie mark was the approximation of 350 degrees. After a few months there, if you had given me a different oven without a Sharpie mark I couldn't have baked shit. Like a lot of ovens, especially ones that are as old as time, this one had hot spots. This meant that certain parts of the oven were hotter than others. For example, the front left was hotter than the front right and the back right. Therefore, approximately halfway through the cooking time you had to turn the trays to get even baking. Next, that charming little oven was cantered slightly forward. This meant that if you were baking something like lemon bars that were liquid going in the oven and solid coming out, they had to be shimmed. What in God's green earth is shimming? I think it's a construction term, but to us it meant you propped up the tray of these now-molten lemon bars with pieces of cardboard to make them level. Sort of the way you prop up that uneven table with a sugar packet in every single shitty diner you've ever been in.

The other ovens had similar issues, with one added bonus: they were low ovens, so you had to bend a lot. Make that two bonuses: the oven on the left was 50 degrees hotter than the oven on the right. We had five mixers. Two were rebuilt or salvaged Kitchen Aid stand mixers, the kind you see in Macy's or vastly overpriced for a chichi color at Williams Sonoma. We also had two larger floor-based mixers, also secondhand, but both worked quite well. Finally, we had the big bread mixer, Big Ed. Since this was Margot's baby for making bread, I never had to deal with that monstrosity. I swear this thing came off a battleship. I mean that literally. Or a freighter. It was huge. How they got it in there, or how the floor joists supported it, I'll never know. It had a clutch to engage the mixing mechanism that was at eye-level with a chipped painted handle. It threw out lubricating oil regularly through one of its orifices, but thankfully I never had to clean that or oil it. The bowl itself weighed about 85 pounds.

The tiny main workspace at Selkirk housed three worktables: one in the center of the main room with a dough sheeter on a table behind it against the wall, and the others in a smaller anteroom that might have been a child's room in the house that it once was. The rest of the space was crammed to the gills with baking racks, shelves with baking tools, and decorative baking supplies. The office was upstairs in the old attic. Aside from the desks for M&M, there were about 300,000 cardboard boxes ready to be folded and adorned with a Selkirk Bakery sticker. I always wondered just how fast that all-wood building packed with ready-to-fold boxes (kindling) would burn. It would be one big Roman candle taking the top off that Victorian in one big *whoosh*. I also wondered how much time we would have to get out.

My day as the morning baker went something like this:

Arise at 4:15, not a minute earlier. Many days, hungover. A few glasses of wine the night before really leave their mark when you keep these kind of hours. Hustle downstairs, make two double espressos, and drink them on the two-minute drive two blocks to the bakery. (Yes, I drove. I know I could have biked or walked. Even better, I drove our Suburban. This is Idaho, USA.) Beat it in the door and haul ass to the time clock to punch in. Turn on the lights, turn on the espresso machine. Fill the sink with hot water and soap. Turn ovens on to their mind-bending configurations: one oven to the Sharpie mark, one oven to 300 degrees, and one to 350 degrees. Unless, of course, I forgot to turn them all on, which happened on occasion.

Now, for real work.

Every morning I made one batch of muffins, rotating daily. These were in addition to pastries that were the same daily, as well as coffee cake. After these came the assorted cookies, cakes and dessert bars for the rest of the day and week. So, on my way to the time clock I glanced at my daily prep list written by Mo, in pencil, on those old-school small yellow lined pads. I was either relieved, or let loose a "Fuck!" to the empty room if it was a big load. I glanced at what the muffin of the day was, although after a year I could tell you even if I were in a coma. Next, it was off to the walk-in to retrieve the pastries that had been rolled out the night before by Margot. If you think the layout of the bakery was quaint, the walk-in looked like it was designed by a kindergartener with attention-deficit disorder. It had a narrow passage, lined on either side by shelves holding fillings and ingredients. About six feet in, it took a hard right, and you had to step down into a tiny space where the baking racks with pastries and cookies were kept. The step went down, but so did the ceiling. This meant that if you were above four feet tall (you must be this high to ride this ride!) you would bash your head or forehead on the ceiling if you forgot to bend over. I cannot tell you how many times I came at that ceiling full throttle because I was in a hurry and damned near knocked myself out. Oh, the words that came out of my mouth then.

Once retrieved, the pastries needed to go into the proof box for about 45 minutes to rise, and the croissants needed to go on the ledge of the oven with the door open. You might ask, "Why would the croissants go onto the oven ledge and not in the proof box?" Well, I could tell you that they were temperamental, that they needed a kiss of warmth to get going and then they went into the proof box. I could tell you that baking yeast products is an art and that everything like temperature and humidity makes a difference. Some mornings in winter, the bakery would be nipple-hardening cold and others in summer would be sweat-inducing without the ovens even being on. But the real reason they went on the oven door is because I was told that's where they went.

Once the pastries were safely proofing, my focus turned to the muffins. Depending on the muffin type (some of those little bastards had a lot of ingredients; I loathed coming in Mondays—Morning Glory day. They contained a shitload of ingredients including freshly grated carrot, with no payoff as they tasted like a shitty good-for-you muffin.). I could get the muffins in the oven just in time to egg wash and top the pastries. With the muffins and pastries baking, it was on to the coffee cake, that, being a daily item, I could do in my sleep. Once all breakfast items were baked it was time to glaze the pastries, which entailed sticking my entire mitt in a mixture of powdered sugar and water that had the texture of loose snot. It sounds simple, but there was a technique. You had to quickly drizzle back and forth, with open fingers, or the sugar snot would roll out of your hands and glob onto the pastries in a thick stream. Although it dried somewhat translucently, Margot could see bad glaze lines from 20 paces. Once that was all done, it was time to put them on a platter and send them out. The takeaway from all of this is that I had to bust my balls to get this finished by the 7:30am opening time.

After this wind sprint, it was time to feed the sours. By sours, I mean the sourdough starters that Margot had coddled since the beginning of time. Or at least a few years. Hated this job. I'm not sure why, exactly. It wasn't that hard.

You mixed one cup of the appropriate flour (rye, wheat, or white) and one cup of water into the starter bucket. Then it was mixed in with a tool that had a spiral wired top that I imagined the Marquis de Sade invented. Then you carefully used a spatula to clean the sides of the plastic bucket to prevent Margot from having a seizure. Everybody in the bakery knew when it was time to feed the sours, since I would carry the buckets with my back bent, in my best Marty Feldman/Igor imitation from *Young Frankenstein*. "Must feed the sours for the mastah!" I would yell. I think I might have been the only person in the entire bakery who thought this was funny, but I did it every single day that I worked there. I have a theory: if it's not funny the first time, it might be funny the 100th. This is similar to my experience with the movie *Caddyshack*. I walked out the first time I saw it. By the 20th time, it was genius.

After feeding the sours, it was off to the various cookie doughs or dessert bars that we carried. These could be Nanaimo bars, or lemon bars, or Rocky Road bars. You get the idea. Repetitious, boring, mind-numbing work. Since my brain is the type that likes constant activity (not to the point of being a Type A asshole, but I like to be engaged), this was the time when I looked around for things or people to screw with. Mostly it meant carrying on long, gossip-filled conversations with Mo, who was working eight feet or so to my left on her own table. Sometimes it meant calling local radio station trying to win tickets to one of their concerts I had no desire of attending. But more often than not, it meant messing with Margot. She was not there yet since she worked afternoons, and I was, therefore, brave. These antics consisted mostly of childish stuff, but I enjoyed the hell out of it:

We had a list posted on the bulletin board on that same first-grade yellow note pad that said "To order." Of course, the list's contents normally were meant to be something like flour or doilies or hazelnuts. But I would scribble, using my left hand to disguise my writing (crafty am I), things like "4 steel-belted radials, preferably Goodrich" or "blue stapler" or "40lbs of veal." Things like that. Just to screw with that perfectionist mind of hers. The next morning I would typically find it erased, or scratched off. A real victory meant an entirely new list replaced it.

Another way I entertained myself was that I would write something profound on Margot's white board, reserved for her own production schedule and special orders. Things like: "Abandon all hope ye who enter here." Or maybe something not so profound—a fake order that on first glance seemed real, and extremely difficult: "200 mini brioche, pickup [next day] at 2pm" (only a couple of hours after she got there). These I did not do so often. Poking the bear was fun, but you had to assess the limits. Other times, I would mess with her utensils. She had a little lime green embroidered and beaded drawstring bag that she hung from a pushpin on a recipe- and postcard-laden bulletin board. The bag held measuring spoons, a thermometer, and a pencil among other things, and had a note attached: "Do not touch upon penalty of death! This was *irresistible!* I touched it many times every day. Nothing really bad, I just reorganized the items or moved the bag a few inches. Just enough.

Since Margot worked the evening shift and stayed well past closing, she would discover mistakes and leave us our very own corrective action plan. Margot was blunt and less than charming in most of her verbal encounters. But in writing? Well. She would scrawl quaint notes like "Burnt!" on something that was overdone. This was a note left for me one day in the walk-in on top of, yes, a tray of browner than usual blondies: "These blondies are awful! Unservable!" Now, anyone who had worked at the bakery for a while and was somewhat comfortable in their job knew all about these notes and how to take them. Me, I would roll my eyes when I found one, and then promptly throw it away, unless it really ticked me off and then I'd respond. The folks I felt sorry for were the new hires, or some of the meeker, nicer girls on the staff. Then I would get really pissed. I would try to coach them and tell them about the boss (and as sure as the sun rises each day, Margot was the boss). I would try to get them to ignore these little diatribes. Occasionally they would cry, although that was rare, but more likely they would live in fear until she arrived for the day. If I happened to be there when she arrived, meaning my day was especially long and already in the shitter, I'd try and look for her car to pull up and warn the minions.

"Gird your loins!"

This I would shout two or three times, one of my favorite lines from *The Devil Wears Prada*. After that we would all become like church mice, and under no conditions look up from our work. Just like they teach you here in Idaho when encountering a bear on a trail. Do Not Look Them In The Eye.

FOURTEEN

....

K-PAX

Margot was just one of the cast of characters at the bakery. M&M were so good-natured, or desperate, that it was a rare thing for anyone to be fired. Many employees were friends or part-time employees who could only work one or two shifts a week.

There was Joanie, a friend of Mo's who lived in the neighborhood. I really don't know how she carved out a living. She worked twice a week for a few hours. Her other job was some sort of vague student advisor-type thing, also part time. She was literally *never* on time the entire time I worked there. It drove me crazy as I flashed back to my old food service manager days, but I ultimately calmed myself down, telling myself that this was someone else's problem. When I discovered later that Joanie liked her marijuana, this explained a lot. She was a blast to work with, though: quick to laugh, and she loved to bitch about anything and everything. This was right up my alley. The German in me follows authority without question, but I do like some bitching with my goosestepping. And since all the mistakes Joanie made, possibly due to being baked herself the entire time, were not my concern, we got along famously. I found her hot buttons about problems in the bakery, or life in general, and happily pushed play and let the music flow.

There was a girl who worked the counter whose name was Lacy. She was a sweet thing, and quick at whatever she was doing. She was so shy, though, and so innocent, that I had to tone my act down considerably around her. At least until she got to know my sense of humor, and even then I was careful about letting the F-bombs fly. My policy at work is the same as life in general: I like to joke around 99% of the time. If I am being serious, something is very wrong. I only joked around with her sporadically, except for the time I tried to scare her early Halloween morning when she arrived. Still dark that early in the morning, I turned off all the lights and left the door ajar. I assumed that a hundred-year-old Victorian with no lights on and with a door ajar on a rainy fall morning might elicit pause. I did not anticipate that someone who is raised in a small town is akin to an animal from a wildlife sanctuary: danger? What danger? Had I pulled this stunt in San Francisco, police would have been called. Instead, Lacey breezed in and headed straight for the light panel. I bellowed, "Good morning Lacey!" Unperturbed, she moused, "Good morning," and we began our duties.

And then there was Kris.

Kris was the counter person in the mornings, and on meeting him, I was struck by a feeling I don't get from many people, at least not at first: this was a good-natured human being. He was a boisterous Oompa Loompa, almost as wide as he was tall. The first few days of working with him proved uneventful enough. He warned me on the proper "Selkirk way" to wash dishes; evidently there was more than one way. But he did it in a way that was without agenda; he was merely showing a new con how they do it on the inside. Kris was also quick to laugh, exactly my age, and shared my love of reading and movies. He pointed out to anyone who would listen that he was, in fact, named after that over-sized elf to the north, so his girth was apropos. He was also a self-imposed homeless person. He had been close to signing a lease for an apartment once, but at the last minute couldn't pull the trigger and sign the lease. This was crazy. Who was willingly homeless? I think it's fair to say, and I'm no statistician, but NO ONE. And to be homeless in the northern climate of Sandpoint? Crazy-er.

Despite being homeless, Kris never actually slept out in the elements. One reason was that he was a regular house sitter. In fact, he was booked most of the year. He would not only stay in the house, but would also garden and take care of pets. He had a way of speaking to problem pets that was other-worldly. He told me that he could sense their energy and communicate with them spiritually. When I heard this bit of news I realized that this man, named for an elf, was special.

He also had a fraternal twin, a sister named JoJo who worked the graveyard shift at the local 7-Eleven. Kris would spend his days after his morning shift visiting friends at the laundromat, hanging out at the local library, or later, visiting Jojo. All of this ground he covered on his custom-made bicycle, which I called his "steed" and dubbed Rocinante. He did not drive, although he did have a license. On the one occasion he drove while we worked together, he used a minivan from the house he was sitting at the time. He broke off the driver's side mirror. I never saw him drive again.

Working together was a daily party. Much to Margot's dismay, Mo would allow us to listen to our own music on a portable music player rather than the usual dismal as shit, good for you jazz or classical music that was supposed to be the bakery's playlist. I played DJ, since Kris hadn't reached the point of buying an iPod, as off the grid as he was. We had similar music tastes, although he didn't like too much of the newer stuff that my kids had turned me on to. So I would happily put together four- or five-hour playlists to last our entire morning shift. We started at 5am or so, when Kris arrived to open the serving area, with softer stuff, often story-based songs like the "Wreck of the Edmund Fitzgerald" and gradually make our way through to the electric early 80s soul that I loved in high school. After opening time came, the music would tone back down and then vary from soft rock to maybe The Partridge Family or classic Cher. More often than not, when a song came on we would yell across the bakery, "I LOVE THIS SONG!" It was a blast.

Part of the reason Kris and I got along so well was that we shared a similar work ethic and attention to customer service. He often pointed out that despite his corpulence, he was quite agile and quick—and he was. He could burn through a line of customers and rarely required help, save the week he lost his glasses and couldn't see the cash register buttons. There and then he decided to cure his vision problems on his own through concentration alone. He was special. He was also back in glasses a week later, and back to his old form.

It was during one of these early morning song sessions that Kris casually told me that he was an alien. OK, maybe he was not that blunt, at least not at first. I think our talks over the weeks about metaphysical topics like the power of intention made him realize I was pretty open-minded. And I knew *he* was pretty New-Agey since he spent hours and many dollars at the local rock and gem store, and had worked there prior to the bakery. He told me breezily about crystals and how they toned to him, and he even bought me some beautiful rocks that had spoken to him and instructed him that they were mine and mine alone.

But rocks are a far fucking cry from another space race.

At the time he told me this bit of news I was making coffee cake and he was wrapping cookies in cellophane. He explained that he and a friend had been out at Snow Creek Falls (one of the many gorgeous waterfalls in Northern Idaho) and a spaceship had appeared in the sky and landed. He knew this spaceship, it belonged to one of his people. One of his friends from his other race, Ramadan, (or was it Xanthamus?) had flown to Sandpoint—or rather the Deep Creek area near Naples, Idaho—to meet him. Ramadan had emerged from the ship to talk to them, and promptly flew away.

I smiled and nodded while creaming butter and sugar in anticipation of adding eggs to start the coffee cake batter.

Pre-measure dry ingredients.

Cream butter and sugar.

Add eggs and vanilla.

Add dry ingredients to wet. Mix.

HOLD IT.

Did I hear that right? Kris was an alien? Like ET phone home? Yes. It's a funny thing about being up that early in the morning. Four-thirty in the morning is an ungodly hour that bends time and experiences in a way that makes remembering them later kind of like looking at a movie that you starred in. But this. Really?

This shit was awesome.

As time went by, I learned a lot about Kris, his friends, and his sister. It seems that being an alien who could communicate with pets on a different plane was just the tip of the supernatural iceberg. There was no area of the magical realm or the celestial arts that Kris wasn't versed in. Tarot? Check. Astrology? Yessir. Horoscopes? You bet your ass. He had been a Shaolin monk before Shaolin Monks were cool.

The time he told me that our entire human race was formerly blue in color, I almost shit myself. Part of me thought that this revelation came from the fact that the movie *Avatar* was in theaters at the time. It seems both he and Jojo were formerly blue in color. I imagine blue is difficult to match clothing with, but apparently when you are royalty you have your own uniform. Jojo, it turned out, was also a queen of the blue people. All that time I was in the presence of royalty and didn't know it.

Ramadan often made appearances for Kris, although I never saw him; *that* is something I would not soon forget. He referred to him and his other advisors from different realms collectively as "the posse." The posse regularly visited and advised. It was about this time that I started thinking. Who does Kris remind me of? I mean, someone who is really bright, lucid, but says things that sound crazier than a shithouse rat. Someone from the movies. Someone that you weren't really sure at the movie's end how things really played out. Yes! He was exactly like Kevin Spacey's endearing character, K-PAX. From then on Kris became K-PAX to me. I even told him that, and being Kris, he loved it.

As a formerly blue alien who spoke with animals and was versed in every form of the transcendental arts, it came as no surprise that K-PAX told me he could read people's auras. Here was the other reason he always had a roof over his head: when he wasn't house sitting, he stayed with numerous friends who required this mystical skill. On one occasion, K-PAX was discussing a consultation he'd had with a couple of friends. Through aura analysis, he deduced what was going on with them, what kind of spiritual and other damage had been done to them, and I don't what the hell else. But I remember it was a lot. He told me that my natural aura was orange. Cool. I like orange, always have. Anyway, he told me that he also did "corrections" of auras. I surmised this was similar to a chiropractic correction. This was often what he did on these overnighters: a consultation with a correction. Even though he didn't charge for his services, people paid handsomely in donations. Two or three hundred bucks a throw. Wowee. But K-PAX didn't intrude on people's auras if he wasn't asked. That's why he didn't try to correct mine; he didn't want to offend. One day, though, he asked me if I wanted him to correct my aura. Hell yes! So K-PAX backed up a step and with a very earnest look on his face, one of deep concentration, he raised an arm and stretched out his hand, his palm open toward me, similar to a spiritual traffic cop. Seriously, I am not making this shit up. And in 10 seconds he opened his eyes.

All done.

If I were you, dear reader, I would want to know how it felt. What happened? Well, like most complicated solutions, the results of an aura correction don't always manifest at once. Once I learned about aura corrections, the shelter he often received after a session, and the corresponding cash flow, it dawned on me: K-PAX was outsmarting us all. Along with the house sitting gigs replete with pet whispering, he was getting paid to have a roof over his head and getting a little spiff at the same time. Brilliant.

There is an interesting thing about K-PAX and his powers, other than being lucky as hell at the lottery, which he played when the posse told him. All of the seemingly crazy shit that he talked about ended up being true. Or most of it. I've also thought about the things people around the world, many who commit atrocious acts, believe. If you stop to think about it, is being a blue alien that far off? At least this alien was non-violent. In fact, I discussed K-PAX and his powers with Mo's husband, an exceedingly bright cynic, who, like Mo, was retired from the Santa Cruz post office. He said, "You know Duke, it's the damnedest thing. You can't disprove anything he says, and all of his shit seems to come true." And so far, and in the following few months, he was right.

My end to the bakery story was benign enough: I injured my back. Although I had preexisting back issues, there is no doubt that this last injury came about due to all the bending and lifting that I did at work. The Idaho workmen's compensation people saw it differently. The great red state of Idaho ranks almost dead last in school funding and probably first in denying workmen's compensation claims, although I have nothing to base this opinion on and am too lazy to do any research. So, I left the fun of working with Mo and the gals in the morning, being part of the town gossip hub, and K-PAX and our early morning light-bending sessions.

Shortly after my bakery chapter came to a close, so did K-PAX's. The bakery sold to new owners a little bit after I left. I knew it was for sale and a couple of pigeons had been circling. I say pigeons not because it was a bad deal; indeed, it was one of the few investments in restaurants in Sandpoint that I would have considered. I say pigeons because you have to be nuts to own a small business in Sandpoint, especially in retail. An acquaintance of mine has tracked the number of restaurants that have changed hands over the past 20 years or so. It is a gaudy number: more than 200, and that is no exaggeration. Really, the only people who make money in the restaurant business in Sandpoint are the realtors who sell them over and over again.

When K-PAX announced to me that the sale was imminent, he also told me that the posse had advised him that his time was near an end at the bakery. While this prediction was ominous, it was by no means earth-shattering. When businesses change hands some employees don't make it for any variety of reasons. I knew a couple of the new owners and they were nice folks and seemed pragmatic enough, so I didn't think a sweeping layoff was in the cards. Still the posse had prophesied after all.

Within a couple of weeks, Kris found himself out of work.

I think the problems were twofold. First, the new owners should have told K-PAX what a treasure he was. Not to mention they should have listened to us, the former employees. I frankly told them Kris was one of the best counter people I had ever seen, let alone one of the best in pure customer service. Despite his visions and conversations with gem stones, he remembered everyone's orders, made excellent coffee, and was a whirling dervish.

The second mistake they made was that one or two of the new owners were helplessly lost, yet one compounded this by his know-it-all posturing, and the other compounded it by simply being in the way. There is a flow to a restaurant or cafe, much like a dance. If I am doing the Hustle, or maybe the Macarena, and you are doing the grade school Sway-and-Feel, this spells trouble on the dance floor. Kris did not take to this well, as I knew he wouldn't. He was not, and never has been, meek. He did not respond with a stiff upper lip. No, his lips worked fine, berating the new owners, and no surprise here, was summarily released of Danish duty.

The posse is always right.

FIFTEEN

····································

WE HAVE GIVEN UP

It is July, and I am writing last year's Christmas letter. That is how things go around here. As I am writing, it is to our very own daily soundtrack. I hear incessant sirens. This is impossible: Sandpoint only has about three sirens per day, and these belong to ambulances on their way to one of the nursing homes on the outskirts of town. These sirens belong to Grand Theft Auto, the crystal meth of video games where our boys aspire to become drug kingpins or just general thugs whose whole goal is to steal cars, run people over, beat them with nine irons, or to just generally FUCK SHIT UP. I swell with pride. I hear the alternate clanging of Brisket's chain collar against his bowl and the pock-pock that is partially chewed kibble hitting the floor. In his gustatory glee he mulches it and simultaneously spills it out of his big maw. Providing a bass note, the pipes in the walls fill and whoosh as the boys' upstairs toilet flushes in one of the many major symphonic movements of the day. In fact, the only activity they will leave GTA for is to use the shitter. "Going to drop a deuce!" they announce. And the time they spend in there: it's a lot. They could finish *The Old Man and the Sea* in the time it takes to get the deed done. What are they doing in there? Any scenario is disconcerting. Quiet comes only from the cat, dreaming of this summer's squirrel that was only playing dead, and Kim, curled up like a cat, sipping tea and reading and tuning out all this crap.

This Christmas letter has been my chore on and off for the past 15 years. It is never on time, nor is it even guaranteed to be yearly. The "letter" was conceived in direct response to the treacly, nausea-inducing letters that we all get from friends we once knew at some point in our lives, but could not identify now in a police line-up. Our letter, we decided, would tell it like it is, without varnish. As age has beset my memory, I now rely on our computer's hard drive to dredge up memories and activities from pictures taken during the past year that I can then bore friends and acquaintances with.

For this year's/last year's Christmas letter, I did the same. Trolling through the images, I found: selfies. Lots and lots of selfies. A veritable treasure trove of self-love. Pouting selfies. Smiling selfies. Tough guy selfies. The most popular? Flexing selfies. Flexing selfies in nature. Flexing selfies on the go. Flexing locker room selfies. They say the hardest thing for a 50-year-old man to do is to remember what he was like as a teenager. But I can-

not remember ever liking my body enough to take giga-
bytes of photos of it.

They are, indeed, all teens, and as teen males they eat
like Viking marauders. They began to stink a few years
ago. Since the Internet has made porn so accessible, I do
not want to ponder their tastes there, except for our
middle son who favored girl-on-girl action as far back as
the 7th grade. (Talking to him about this was easily the
most traumatic and embarrassing conversation either of
us has had, with or without each other.) I discovered the
goods one morning as he was still in bed—later than
usual—with our beat-up old laptop. As I walked over to
his bed I found him staring at his Lionel Messi screen-
saver. Odd. He was an avid soccer fan at the time, but
staring at a screen saver? Then I noticed the tent pole in
his sheets. I decided, with not-so-gentle prodding from
Kim, that this was my area of responsibility: walking him
through the horrors of looking at porn. *Hypocrite!*

I chose the local Starbucks to impart my wisdom. To
this day, he cannot walk inside that particular Starbucks,
he only uses the drive-through. He sat there the entire
time divining the grain pattern in the table while I
creepily stumbled through my lecture. The conversation
is a bit of a blur, but I do remember advising him how to
properly dispose of the evidence, among other things. A
Norman Rockwell moment it was not. Horrible. Hard as
that was for Jack, it could have been worse. A few years
after this happened, the mother of one of Jack's friends
found a porn site on her son's phone. It seems he was

skilled enough to find it, but not to delete the browser history. She then made him *watch the entire video with her.* This was pure genius. We now do our own version of this. When we hear slang that we have never heard and ask the kids, we watch for a scintilla of discomfort followed by their unwillingness to explain. Kim then looks up the offending term on her phone using Urban Dictionary. She then reads it aloud. Having your mother define "motor boating" or the "eiffel tower" empties the room *fast.*

As male teenagers, they have a great admiration for boobs and other lady parts. As a heterosexual male of the species, I concur. Like many males who might not freely admit it, the boys make many important decisions, like what television show or movie to watch, based on the level of nudity. And when it occurs, hooting, hollering, and comments ensue. Feminists, please, do not write me letters. I am married to a very centered woman, who has taught them how to properly handle a woman: with the fear she is due. I am just a little annoyed. I had to spend hard-earned summer money to purchase a subscription to *Playboy Magazine,* and convince my parents to take me to the "R" movie with "the amazing plot". Now, nourishing nudity is but a click or streaming device away. The only thing that trumps boobs is a live sporting event. I jest. Nothing trumps boobs.

Aside from a passion for breasts, the other thing they have in common is that they all cherish getting the last word in, or absent of that going for the ruthless remark.

We recently took a family portrait—which, as is the case with all family portraits—I assume was the alpha female's idea. The portrait sitting had its very own soundtrack, much to the dismay of our photographer:

Austin: "Wow, nice smile, you douche."

Sam: "Fuck off Austin. At least I'm not going to lose my hair when I'm 20."

Jackson: "Are those girls pants you're wearing Sam? Are they riding up your crotch enough?"

Jackson: "Look at Sam's hands. What a freak. What are you, a cowboy? Are you asking for chaps for Christmas?"

Sam: "You're a bitch, Jack."

Me: (*whispering*) "Boys! Shut the fuck up."

Yes indeed. An F-Bomb was dropped at a family photo session. It was dropped by a 13-year-old and his responsible 50-year-old father. That is not only because his brothers were being pricks, and being the youngest he has to strike back, but also because, simply, *we have given up*. Somewhere along the line, we've effectively given the green light to our sons cursing around the house. We've largely thrown in the towel for two reasons: a) we trust our sons to act respectfully around adults, and b) We (I) find it a bit hypocritical to enforce a no-cursing rule when I, on occasion, throw out some doozies. After all, they didn't learn this in a vacuum. It really is liberating. That might be the wrong word, but you know what I mean: no more worrying about dropping the random "Fuck!" when you stub your toe, or the cat barfs in his bowl that sits on the kitchen counter right next to the coffee machine. It sits there, by the way, so that the crowned prince of stupidity, the dog, doesn't suck down the cat's food as well as his own, nor sadly can he dispatch of said vomit. We've allowed the cursing largely by not protesting against it. A sin of omission, so to speak. To plagiarize Anthony Bourdain, the men in our house use curse words largely as punctuation. OK. It might not be that bad, but it's a far cry from the adorable gurgling of a three-month-old infant.

Oh, but dear reader, allowing foul language is not the only way we've given up. After all of these years, our house is still an eyesore. Sure, we've made some improvements. We've slapped on some interior paint, added some furniture, fixed a few things. But not all. We have given up trying to plug the dike, choosing instead to hope our house will still be standing when these animals we like to call sons leave for college, and the ball of hair that we like to call our dog finally shuffles off his mortal coil. Until those fantasies are realized, our house runs like this:

Kim gets up at around 4:40 to get to the gym by 5am. I know, this is deranged behavior. Inevitably, if her stupid watchette doesn't wake me up, her plodding around in the closet does. (It is a watchette because the band broke off her Nike digital watch and she is too cheap or too lazy to replace it. She just keeps the face and amputated straps on the nightstand.) I normally try and get up by 5:30 to suck down some coffee and read the newspaper online. I also must feed the cat that, with his full winter coat looks like he has swallowed Rhode Island, and the dog, who waits dutifully for his kibble and its dusting of parmesan cheese.

Jackson, our middle son, gets up at 6:15, plugs in his phone to the portable speaker in the master bathroom and starts blaring whatever is on the playlist for that particular day. All the while he pours ungodly amounts of shampoo into his hair and slathers on the Old Spice body wash that was a stroke of genius marketing to teenage boys. The bathroom becomes a veritable Phil Spector "wall of smell." Sam rolls groggily down the stairs for his morning dose of ESPN at around the same time Austin, in full zombie mode, walks to his shower. He showers in the boy's bathroom, with its toothpaste-caked sink, towel rack without a rod, and toilet that gets cleaned quarterly. The other boys, and anyone else in the neighborhood it seems, use our master bathroom. This last point requires Kim, when she gets home from the gym, to position towels around the glass-walled shower so as not to flash the kids. A woman needs privacy after all. Once showered, the boys get dressed and start the daily hunt for socks. The sock basket is hell on earth. It's like it was designed as some sort of Greek mythology punishment: instead of Sisyphus and his boulder, there is a basket of socks that nary have a match. They seemingly are all different sizes, styles and colors. Not one match in the group. Then, if you do find a match, holes in the toes. Do those get thrown away? No.

They get dumped back in the basket for the next poor schlub to find.

Once dressed, the two older boys pack their lunches (these are largely snacks. We have given up on proper nutrition as well) and eat breakfast. Sam chooses this moment, exactly 29 minutes before they need to leave for school, to shower and primp and admire his hair. This is not as easy as it sounds. He really likes his hair. And he really likes his showers: he must unwind after a grueling 11-hour slumber. Often he must wait for bathroom time, since Jack occupies the mirror with his self-adoration society as long as possible. Breakfast for the boys typically amounts to the previous night's dinner. We have somehow made this transition: it offends our boys, and I do not misuse that term, if they need to lower themselves to cereal. Much better and easier to microwave something. By some miracle, they make it out the door 10 minutes prior to school starting, normally fighting the entire time. The timing works since school is a half-mile away.

Austin, the eldest, is the driver, despite the fact that Jackson is now also eligible. He has always been responsible, adhering to that cliché about first-borns. He wields the power of the first-born comfortably—in fact, helping us parent on a regular basis, apparently disdainful of our abilities. Once in the car, it is imperative that he plug in his phone to pick the appropriate playlist for the drive of less than 5,000 feet. Of course he could care less what time his brothers need to be at school. At his age, the solar system has changed its rotation, disregarding the sun completely in favor of circling him. He now attends the high school, after a brief hiatus at the hometown charter school. It was not his scene. I'm not sure about other charter schools, but I have a feeling many are like ours: a continuation for many of the Waldorf or Montessori school systems and the like; or, the beginning of formal education for children who had been home-schooled. These are those schools where the kids call the teachers by their first names. They're like the New Age religions that "gather" instead of "congregate" and sing rock and roll songs instead of hymns. Not wrong, necessarily. Certainly there is a place for them. But places where I feel nervously uncomfortable.

Jackson, despite his innate ability to boss and bully his younger brother—easy because he has at least 30 pounds on Sam—nevertheless defers to his older brother, giving him all the time in the world to pick his perfect song, seething all the while. Despite being roughly the same size as Austin, I suppose he defers to him because he owes Austin: he has blazed the trail for Jack since kindergarten. Perhaps this is the reason it is difficult for Jackson to initiate a conversation with anyone in a position of authority. Anyone. It could be a teenage store clerk in some trendy clothing store, or a young bank teller at our local bank where his own mother works. He simply cannot ask them to open a changing room for him, or get cash from his account. Jack could be afloat in a life raft for months, starving, but once he

hit land he couldn't ask a server for a fork at his welcome back banquet. I am not sure if this is a symptom of
our current youth as a whole—they grow up texting and
looking at screens, offering up any amount of personal
information online, yet cannot order a cheeseburger
from a stranger—or if it is some peculiar flaw exclusive
to him. This is despite the fact that he is so charming
and gregarious that he earned the nickname "the mayor"
in grade school. He has charm in bucket loads, and we
suspect he knows this so we have begun encouraging
him to use his powers for good.

Jack is also, quite literally, the laziest person alive. If it
didn't require a needle, I am certain he would submit to
an IV feeding to prevent any possible exertion. This is
an exaggeration, but not by much. He leaves cups, towels, sweatshirts, bowls of ramen scraps and anything else
where he drops them and forgets they are there. He even
managed to leave his well-worn football pads in his can-
vas gym bag in his room in our un-air conditioned
house for the summer. By August, I thought a beast of
burden had wandered upstairs to his room and died. Between his slovenliness and his early love of adult cine-
ma, I believe Jack could petition early admission to any
fraternity at any college in America.

Sam most certainly does not sit quietly waiting for
his older brother's music choice. Even though he sits
squarely in the crosshairs of his two older brothers, he
gives as good as he gets. He has used his brief time on
this planet wisely, honing his barbs. In fact, with his re-

marks, singing, and nicknames, he makes his brothers crazier than shithouse rats. It is both ingenious and expedient: he makes up for his lack of muscle mass with a sharpened vocabulary. The pen, they say, is mightier than the sword. For some reason, perhaps because his birth order is last, he must be first everywhere else. Out of the car. In line at dinner. Anywhere. He also tries to differentiate himself from his brothers. While they all ski, Sam is into "park skiing," which combines danger and injury with the category of skier considered to be the most ill-mannered and disliked on the mountain. He sits in the back of the car, headphones on, ready to launch a verbal assault while being far enough away to avoid physical danger.

When the boys come home, shirts come off, pajama bottoms go on. They quickly morph into locusts looking for anything and everything to eat. Wait. That's not accurate. They look for anything and everything to eat that satisfies *their definition* of what an after-school feeding should include. To qualify as an appropriate snack it must be: a) easy to prepare, ideally emptied out of a bag; b) different every single day; c) salty and/or crunchy; and d) filling. I have just described the yeti of snacks, ones that do not exist, at least in our house. They do exist at fast food restaurants. Once the boys discovered Taco Bell, one of a handful of fast food franchises in town, they fell madly and hopelessly in love. They asked me a few times at first if they could have money to get a few tacos after school, to which I laughed before I lectured:

"Snacks are not a right, they are a luxury! Snacks are intended to be a healthy tide-you-over until dinner! I am most certainly not buying you an extra meal in the middle of the day! Do I need to remind you dinner is just a couple of hours away? There is fruit on the counter!"

When they stopped non-listening, they pooled their money and went anyway. Jackson, smitten more than the other two and flush from his paint store job, proceeded to spend $180 *in one month* making runs to the border, before he came to his senses. In the absence of fast food, they resort to ramen, something Kim and I parented them away from only to have our flanks overcome by their numbers. But theirs is not just ramen made in the classic sense. No broth for them. No, to be made correctly in our house, ramen must be cooked in the microwave in a bowl of water to be drained and then tossed with the included pack of dyed-brown monosodium glutamate and a fistful of butter. Snacks are consumable entertainment.

And every evening I make dinner. Since I have a restaurant background, at some point I think I might have liked to cook. That has given way to drudgery, but it has not stopped me from varying dinners. Partly because I get bored easily, partly because we rarely eat out, and partly because the leftovers disappear at breakfast. Because of this, and because I cannot stand answering the same questions over and over, I make a weekly menu and post it on the door to the basement. But heaven forbid I put something on the menu that is not interesting or up to their now high standards. Should I list something like tuna casserole or tuna melts, I get the stink-eye from everyone, and inevitably the question: "Tuna melts? Are you guys going out?" Or, on occasion the comment: "Tuna casserole? You're really phoning-in this one, Dad." I post it on the basement door because it is adjacent to my home office, and I can then watch their reactions. Not the positive ones, those are only a little satisfying. It's the negative reactions that are worth it. And if they are consistently negative—most of these belong to Sam—I then name the dish after the person: Sam's Split Pea Soup. Sam's Minestrone. Sam's Green Curry Chicken.

Another battle we lost long ago, or rather we simply threw in the towel, was that of eating at the dinner table as a family. Yes, I know, I've read those same reports. And yes, we are doomed. But we choose to eat dinner in front of the TV, eating off of the world's cheapest metal folding TV trays that I picked up long ago at Wal-Mart for $3 each. Actually, we have had to replace a couple, which I have done by getting some nifty superhero trays on eBay. I am 50 years old and I eat off of an "Iron Man!" TV tray every night made for a four-year-old. But my drinks don't slide since I have a ready-made indentation for my big boy glass.

DUKE DIERCKS

SIXTEEN

·····································

I SEE WHITE PEOPLE

I excel at generalizations and unfairly lumping people into groups. I started honing these skills, as most of us did, in high school. Over the years, I have become quite good at it. Normally it takes a few years in a new place to decide how to categorize people, and after living in Sandpoint and the Idaho Panhandle for a dozen years, I feel qualified to divide Sandpoint into the following major groups:

Old-Growth Hos: These people were born and raised in Sandpoint. Many are descendants of town founders or early big shots. Their names adorn streets and parks. In most cases, the hillbilly has been bred out of them, but they still fly their Ho flags proudly.

Old Hos/Hillbillies: These are the live-off-the-land types. They normally live on larger tracts of land, proudly display their NRA stickers in the windows of their trucks that, unlike city dwellers, are actually put to good use. They believe their land is their land and they should be allowed to do with it what they damn well want. They believe that if junior is old enough to walk, he is old enough to learn how to shoot. Many also have multitudes of motorized toys: all-terrain vehicles or motorcycles for summer months, and snowmobiles for tearing it up in the winter. The really serious ones? They go mud-bogging in their specially souped-up trucks that require a step ladder to get in.

Conspiracy Theorists: These are the tinfoil-hat types that believe the inevitable black helicopters are days away from landing. The government is evil, and is out to get us. I don't know what percentage of these people are survivalists or doomsday preppers, but I would put the number close to 100%. Yes, some people here actually are preparing for the end of days, Armageddon, or the Rapture. I hope they are wrong, or my family will die eating out-of-date olives, anchovies, and relish.

Live Here to Live Here Types: These people moved to Sandpoint to enjoy the lifestyle: skiing in the winter, boating, hiking and composting in the summer, and being poor year round. They hold multiple jobs to allow them the freedom to live here. Typically they are clothed in natural fibers, use bikes for transit, shop at the farmer's market and are experts on craft beers.

New Growth Progressives: These tend to be transplants, many from the C-word state, bringing their crazy ideas with them and threatening to poison the pristine gene pool of Idaho. (They also are educated, help drive up property values with the purchase of homes, and add to the tax base, but we like to overlook that.) There *are* plenty of locals in this group as well. This group tends to appreciate the area and its beauty, and participate in outdoor activities. While they appreciate the area, they see room for dreaded change and are not afraid of it, regardless of who has the idea.

Generalizations about groups of people are not the only area of sociology where I excel. I also have a keen observational eye that has been refined by living in multiple parts of the country. So I feel qualified here to point out some things that are different or striking about this area, as well as things that you might not encounter in your daily life:

1)   **I see white people.** I mean holy shit, everyone in Idaho is white! Enough so that when I meet, say, an African-American up here, I go out of my way to be overly friendly—gushing to possibly make them feel more comfortable, if they are indeed uncomfortable, or is it just white guilt—and let them know we're not a bunch of racists at this latitude. We're just overly white.

2)   **I see old people.** Yes, I'm sure you do too. You can't escape them, really. But as a proportion of our population, we have a lot, and I'm not sure how they all wound up here. It's like one giant AARP salmon spawn. The thing I find curious is this: aren't they supposed to retire some place warm? Not some place with prime hip-breaking weather conditions?

3) **Bald eagles**. This simply never gets old. They are majestic and huge. Some days you might see a dozen in a tree, some days they might float above your house. One day walking the dog, I saw a large bird in a tree and thought, "What is a chicken doing up in that tree?" It turned out to be a bald eagle. You see, it was a rather large bird and I am a blithering idiot.

4) **Logging trucks**. These damn things rumble through town daily, filled with impossibly large trees and impossibly thin steel rods keeping these trees from flattening your Subaru, the official state car of Idaho. (see #16)

5) **Parking spaces**. No matter where you go, there is likely to be plenty of parking available. So much so that when there is not, people want to take action. The perceived lack of parking in our downtown core has led some of the crustier old bastards to boycott shopping downtown. They forget, I think, the city lot one block away that largely stands half-full, except during the tired 50s car show that we will no doubt have until the boomers die off. They also forget that the trudge into Wal-Mart, where parking is plentiful, is actually farther than the walk to the store from that city parking lot a block away.

6) **Utilitarian fashion**. (See Carhartt #20) We *do* get fashion up here, albeit late. If you happen to see someone wearing the latest fashion, it is as noticeable as a different skin color. These people, often found in their native habitat—Starbucks— are immediately branded as

city folk. We do wear fashions, but they must be functional, like the latest ski apparel, smart wool, or boots. Non-utilitarian fashion, like suede or high heels, is reserved for special occasions, since it's ridiculous to wear things that are susceptible to weather. A snappy flannel ensemble will get you in most places anyway. There is also largely a dearth of makeup here. In that, we are the polar opposite of Dallas or Houston. I think it has something to do with the weather, but that is pure speculation.

7) **Republicans.** We are, I believe, in competition with Wyoming for the "Reddest State in the Union" award. Hoo-rah. Idaho is so red that state and national elections are over largely before they begin. They are over at the exact moment candidates declare their party affiliations.

8) **Auctions and raffles.** Held for anything and everything. Part of being a true red state demands that the state budget be balanced, so there is precious little spending on frivolous things like education. Doubling down on fiscal conservatism is the fact that we live in a relatively poor, sparsely populated area, without the tax receipts of larger areas. ("Poverty with a view" is how some locals describe our area.) So to raise money, there is regularly someone at the entrance of every grocery store raffling candy bars, popcorn, or a half-steer's worth of meat to raise money for something. Auctions for different charities, all with basically the same items, dot the calendar. Car washes raise money for sports teams, and

we have regular votes for school levies to help offset the fact that we are 48th in the country in school spending. Who in the hell are 49 and 50? I guess it's good to be number one at something.

9) **Reinventors.** It is amazing in a small town how effortlessly you can reinvent yourself. There is no one to call bullshit on your new persona. I suppose this is true if you move anywhere else, but it seems that in a small town—at least ours—people accept your cover story more readily. Of course you can't reinvent yourself into a neurologist, but you can make yourself other things. Never owned a restaurant? Well you can become a chef. Just call yourself one. Take a few classes and you can be the massage therapist you always wanted to be. I'm sure part of this comes from need. Jobs are scarce. If you are a professional, i.e. someone who had the foresight and wherewithal to pay attention in class and forego happy hour in favor of graduate school, you have it made. But if, like me, you have a largely untransferable skill set, you need to take action. All of these reinventors seem to follow one type of path: jobs that sound dreamy. They are chefs, artists, interior designers, massage therapists, spa owners, and the occasional life coach. Life coach. Is that really a job? Any good coach will tell you it's the personnel, anyway.

10) **Press secretaries.** These people are typically crazier than shithouse rats; their lives are a mess, yet their message remains upbeat and resolute. They *do*, in fact, act much like the White House press secretaries

who explain away disasters and scandals through semantics, half-truths and the savvy to get their message out first, and force others to disprove it. It is a cuckoo's nest sort of genius. The reason they exist solely in the small town bubble is precisely because since the town is so small, everyone knows all the stories, or has their own town telegraph system to acquire information. In a big city these people would just move on and find new friends. In the small town they must assimilate. Therefore they get their message out quickly, forcefully setting the state-sponsored talking points. They also inherently glom on to newcomers where the bridges still are intact, and whose brains are as empty as newborns. When we moved to Sandpoint, we found ourselves unwittingly suckered in by multiple press secretaries, only to be told by others, or to find out later, that things were not as they seemed. We were just the new idiots in the village.

11) **Elected officials**. Sure, you can see them elsewhere, but here you can see them in-person and, more than likely, you will actually know a few of them. Nowhere is it more true than in a small town: the world is run by people who show up. Local elections are not only decided by a handful of votes, but the entire election only *includes* a handful of votes scribbled on ballots with little miniature golf pencils. I was, in fact, recruited to run for mayor. It was not for my stunning intellect, nor my animal magnetism. No, the person who tried to recruit me seemed to think my haircut (shaved head) was not of necessity, but rather a political statement. I'm not

quite sure what he thought my slogan was going to be. "Hi, I'm Duke, and I'd like to be your skinhead candidate for mayor!" That was a very short recruiting conversation.

12) **Survival rations and survival ration "sales" at the local supermarket.** (See conspiracy theorists.) Yes, we have aisles in our stores that sell industrial-sized #10 cans of powdered eggs and the like. Our town supports two Starbucks and three sushi restaurants, but also supports "Survival Rations Sales" where you can stock up on your very own MREs. We have very interesting demographics.

13) **Thirty-year-old grandmothers.** This is an exaggeration, but not by much. And no, this is not terribly common. But wow.

14) **Wal-Mart.** Oh the wonderful sights to be seen! I have been in other Wal-Marts in other parts of the country, and yes, you do see some amazing things, many of which are now posted online. But our Wal-Mart? Our Wal-Mart is 1080p in a world of analog TV.

15) **Mark Fuhrman.** Yes, that Mark Fuhrman. Ben Stein. Yes, that Ben Stein. We also have a famous movie actor who owns property in the area. It is worth noting that he once visited our restaurant, and despite my stance that he was "just another customer," I proceeded to vomit pleasantries all over him. I am now surprised I didn't whip out my earmarked issue of Tiger Beat for him to sign. My wife thought it was disgusting, and for the millionth time, she was right.

16) Subarus. This is the state car of Idaho. Every other car is a Ru. Unless, of course, you have "made it." Then, you might drive one of those cars from Europe. Most of these are Audis, possibly because they are good in snow, possibly because they are made in European ski country and go with the ski town vibe, but most likely because they seem to be the most low-key of those cars from Europe. Conspicuous consumption largely does not exist here. BMWs? Rare. Mercedes, even more so. Porsches? I think there are five. Without a doubt the go-to luxury SUV for the conspicuous is the Range Rover. Or, for the conspicuous Republican Big Baller, the tricked-out Escalade. There are two Smart Cars in town. The cars themselves are diminutive, but the statement the owners are trying to make is HUGE. A few men do still drive their penises around, but overall Hummers have fallen out of grace.

17) Broken windshields. Almost every car in our area endures a broken windshield, seemingly on a yearly basis. Many people, like us, choose not to get them repaired, at least until they ruin your vision, since they will only happen again. I assume they are due to the "chip and seal" roads we have up here. To get technical, these roads are asphalt with sharp little rocks glued on. I have no idea why; I assume it increases the durability. When these little pebbles inevitably become loose, they are launched by the car in front of you, cracking the glass. I also assume, since this is Idaho, it is a cheaper alternative to a better solution.

18) **Jury-rigging of things.** This is only limited by the imagination and the visionary's supply of duct tape. Here, I am with my chosen people. Broken taillight? *Red duct tape.* Broken window? *Duct tape and a garbage bag.* The best jury-rigging I have ever seen was on a 70s-era GMC Jimmy. The back roof was taken completely off. No front doors. The rear seats had been removed and two children's car seats were bungee-corded in place, offering open air driving for the kiddies. It is perhaps a commentary on this needed skill set that each of our sons has made a wallet out of duct tape for an elementary school project. Teach them while they're young, we say.

19) **Moose.** Plural. These prehistoric looking things lumber through town mostly in winter months when grazing is scarce. They eat old apples off of trees, and in the spring help themselves to newly sprouted gardens. It is amazing to see how fast the sentiment from our citizens turns from "How cute!" to something else entirely. An entire family chose our alley last year to set up camp during the winter. When I chanced upon the mom, while I was out for my morning walk, I ran away like a girl with my confused dog bringing up the rear. The entire spectacle was observed by one of our neighbors while she was having her morning coffee.

20) **Carhartt.** If the Subaru is the state car, Carhartt is the state uniform. Or, absent Carhartt, any and all types of camouflage wear. Wearing camo is not to be limited to hunting. Camo is acceptable in almost any

gathering. I have never seen a camo tuxedo, but I have seen a camo bow tie and cummerbund set. Classy. I have also seen camo bottle openers and other kitchen gear, although I am not sure why you need to blend into the environment when you are opening a bottle of wine.

21) Roadkill permits. Yes. Read it again: Roadkill permits. In our state it is but a click away to generate a permit to harvest the deer that lost his valiant battle with the F-150. You can take it home and eat it, or should you have the wherewithal you can sell it.

22) Obtaining/avoiding roadkill. Before you can tag it, you've got to kill it. Our local drivers education classes specifically teach, as part of the curriculum, how to properly hit a deer, elk, or moose should they jump in front of your car. This is a far cry from my drivers ed teacher, Mr. Perkins, instructing us how to hit a squirrel. But in reality, this is not a joke; these animals can cause great harm. The trick? Accelerate. You need to drive them "up and over" to do the least amount of damage to your vehicle. And when you see one deer, there are likely more.

23) Realtors, churches and dentists. If you stood in town and threw a rock, it would most likely hit one of the three. For churches, we are the Baskin-Robbins of Christian worship here. The number of realtors peaked in 2004 or so, when we received a flurry of national press citing Sandpoint's beauty. Then, everybody and their cousin became an agent, trying to cash in on crazy land values and a market that was on fire, making realtors fully 10% of our population. I made the mistake of commenting on this in a letter to our newspaper. Hell hath no fury like a newly minted realtor scorned. But the amount of dentists is the most curious thing. It begs the question: with so many dentists, where have all the teeth gone?

24) **Lack of news coupled with misspelled news.** I've never checked, but I think our newspaper is six pages long. An automobile wreck is front page news. Our same newspaper is known for daily misspellings. It can be a fun version of "word search" to find the misspelled words. I don't know how other newspapers avoid this problem, but I would assume it has something to do with spell check that every computer on the planet has.

25) **Letters to the editor.** Oh, sure: every newspaper has these. But I dare say none are as entertaining as ours. I could easily fill a book with these gems. Kim thinks that these outspoken letters are akin to the butterfly effect: seemingly small things can have a large impact elsewhere. A very small, vocal group can engineer change in a small town, simply due to the numbers (see elections #10.) This invites loud opinions in the newspaper and elsewhere. In a large city, you might just be a voice in the wilderness. The really funny ones, though, are the ones that tackle national or global problems. Do they not know that neither Congress nor the United Nations subscribes to our newsletter?

26) **Lack of crime.** This is a doozy. A welcome doozy. Very little happens here. And when it does? It

makes the crime blotter in the newspaper. Largely ignored in metropolitan areas, the blotter is a must-read to
see who was arrested for drunk driving or hitting their
spouse. This is Kim's favorite part of the paper; she reads
it like I read the sports, which in a way it is. I can't speak
for all our neighbors, but since crime is largely nonexist-
ent, we do not lock our house. Except the front door at
night. Back door remains unlocked. Figure that out.
When we go to the store for just a few things, we leave
the keys in the ignition.

There are two other things that I experience daily
that you might not. The first is a precious quantity in
more densely populated areas, and that is: Time. It is
amazing how much not commuting, not sitting in traffic,
or not driving miles to the grocery store saves time. We
once met with someone who was relocating from Los
Angeles to Sandpoint. She calculated that she was going
to have three extra hours in her day. The second is this:
Friendly people. I'm not sure how to explain this. Lack of
stress? Fresh air? Delusional thinking? Whatever the
reason, almost everyone you encounter is pleasant and
helpful. This can be tricky, though. Sometimes you have
to stifle the urge to kidney-punch the adorable senior in
line in front of you as she talks to the cashier about her
grandchildren, well after the transaction is complete.

DUKE DIERCKS

SEVENTEEN

....

A PHYSICS LESSON

I didn't take physics, as it seemed like way too much work. In fact, I had a very scientific method for picking classes: if it required a term paper or started before 9am, I did not take the class. It seems remarkable now that I was able to fill so many pages here with word things. Despite my lack of physics knowledge, a quick search on the Internet machine offers this definition of force:

"... a force is that which can cause an object with mass to change its velocity (which includes to begin moving from a state of rest), i.e., to accelerate, or which can cause a flexible object to deform."

My wife discovered what force meant in her own unique fashion. And together we discovered the fabric that makes up a small town.

Although our family skiing as a group had started to wane, possibly due to our boys being in another league than the adults, and possibly due to the fact that Kim and her mom seemed to prefer hot tea, warm fires, and crosswords to smelly locker rooms and freezing temperatures, the whole family nevertheless went skiing on January 15, 2012.

Our ski days were typically ski half-days, partly because the lack of lines at the lifts meant you could get quite a bit of skiing done by noon. Partly. But mostly we did half-days because after a few runs we succumbed to the siren call that was hot chocolate. Hot chocolate, marshmallow treats, and Cheetos to be exact—our usual white trash carb loading. And after sitting in the warm ski lodge, it was hell to get motivated to ski much more. It is pathetic, really. On this day, we chose to take our sustenance at the Outback Restaurant, a log cabin structure cleverly named because it is situated "out" and "back" on Mt. Schweitzer's north bowl. The north bowl has great terrain with a speedy six-person lift, but unfortunately does not connect to the main lodge, locker rooms and parking areas other than by way of one single cat track. For non-skiers, a cat track is a track that the Snowcat grooming machines use, as do ski patrol and other workers on snowmobiles. And in this case, everyone else trying to get down the hill, no matter their ski levels. This creates a bit of controlled mayhem as invincible teens blazing down the path commingle with old farts and tiny tots who are so unfairly light that they need to be pulled, even on a descent. Adding to this stew, the path itself is often rutted from the snowmobile tracks.

As we were making our way down the top third of the path, Kim was skiing directly in front of me. She appeared to catch one of her edges and did a sort of do-see-do, careened off course and awkwardly embraced a metal pole, knee first, in a cloud of powder. This metal pole sunk into the earth was, of course, necessary, as it had to be sturdy enough to bear the weight of the nylon twine it was holding up. Twine. Metal pole. I have often wondered since then what metal poles, buried in the earth, are doing on the side of runs frequented by hundreds of skiers and less than considerate snowboarders. Couldn't it have been plastic netting? Possibly. But then plastic netting, like they use in ski races, would only keep people from going where the mountain says they are not supposed to. Wink. Wink.

Being a considerate husband, I had already started to giggle. Until I heard the screaming.

I stopped where she was and did my best to comfort her. Unfortunately, her mom was there as well and had to watch the whole thing. Unaware, Kim's dad skied by, racing our sons to the bottom. Fortunately, a ski lesson was also returning to the bottom, and I flagged the teacher down to radio ski patrol, which saved time. Once we were at the bottom, Kim was loaded into the waiting ambulance, but not before they had to remove her boot. I asked the ambulance driver, who had been a regular at our restaurant (small town), if they could give her something for the pain. He said they needed to get the boot off and then they would give her something in the ambulance. She was screaming and her mother was crying. The ambulance driver told a mutual friend later that he thought I was going to punch his lights out.

When we arrived at the hospital, the doctor was someone I knew from the health club (small town.) In fact, one of the thriving occupations in Sandpoint, and any ski town, is orthopedic surgeon. No surprise there. He told me that Kim had dislocated her hip. It drove through the bone and out, shattered her shin, and tore an ACL in her knee. Immediate surgery ensued to repair the hip. Knee surgery followed the next day to repair her knee.

During her week-long hospital stay, at our very own Bonner General Hospital, her physical therapist, who was the father of one our son's best friends, noticed that her good knee moved in all sorts of interesting ways, which, while normal for Gumby, was not for a human. The verdict from the ensuing MRI was that the good knee had a torn ACL, and PCL and MCL. Bonus! They would operate on that knee a few weeks later. First, though, she would be discharged to mend a bit prior to that surgery.

Before that could happen, we had to turn our home into the 4077th MASH. This was not without trauma: our sons' Xbox room became the hospital room. We rented a hospital bed from a medical supply rental company that had, naturally, already heard about the accident. This was a small town writ large: when I went to order the bed from people I had never formally met, I came to find out they had the order already waiting, they would drive it over personally that afternoon and set it up, and I could pay for it later. Our local community cancer care charity lent us other essentials like chairs, walkers, and a toilet seat extension that enabled one to void comfortably into a waiting bucket. I know. I'll get to that. Our neighbor promptly ordered her husband and another neighbor who we barely knew to build a ramp off of our back deck to facilitate her wheelchair and any doctor visits.

Once Kim was home, she was bedridden for eight weeks. Only then could she negotiate the stairs using crutches. I know what you're probably thinking: this translated into an extraordinary amount of work for me. I would have to wash her hair, slather lotion on her, and dump her buckets. Sadly, she did not allow me the one thing I was looking forward to: sponge baths. Nevertheless, I forged ahead, our wedding vows looping in my head along with my favorite scenes from the movie *Misery*. Like all things, though, the glass was half-full: I was able to load the dishwasher any old way I felt like, I cut my toenails wherever I pleased, and I got the bed all to myself.

Her recovery after the second knee surgery was difficult, but again was aided by folks who sprang to our aid. At first, the local EMS director, who was on a non-profit board with Kim, gave us free ambulance rides back and forth from the doctor. Later, friends who were physical therapists pitched in to supplement her regular physical therapy and to get her to and from other doctor appointments. They helped get her out of the house, down the ramp, and shoehorn her into our car while snow and ice covered the ground. This was greatly appreciated since getting in and out of a car is tricky if you can't bend your knees or put weight on your legs. Our neighbor who organized the ramp construction also organized round-the-clock visitors and meals while I was away on business. Acquaintances, not necessarily good friends, showed up randomly with meals and magazines to read. On many occasions strangers stopped me in the grocery store to ask about Kim's health, and pass along good wishes. Our local florists, of which we have two, unless you count those sad grocery store flower sections, were able to offer advice to well-wishers what kind of arrangement had not yet been ordered so she would not receive two of the same kind of flower.

And the ski mountain? They responded too. They sent a plant. And two day passes. Not quite what I was expecting for a multi-year season pass holder who blew out her knees and hip bashing into a pole on a crowded all-mountain egress run at the beginning of the season. But plants are nice.

Now she is almost fully recovered. She can't run anymore, and with one ACL still flopping around, her nondreams of playing for the WNBA are shot. She only limps after sitting or standing too long, or strenuous exercise, and her kneeling days are over. That last one stings.

The memories of that day still linger, especially when we ski past that spot. But what lingers for me, a grateful husband, is the outpouring from this community. Could the same thing have happened in a city? Perhaps. But this seems to be part and parcel of the small town experience: you are part of something small that is at the same time large.

It seems daunting now, thinking back on this great adventure that we undertook: moving a family across the country to a town in the wilderness of the Idaho Panhandle, whose population could not fill a sports stadium. Some dark winter days I question our decision. But I guess that second-guessing is not exclusive to just *our* journey. What we were running from on the surface appeared to be (*objects in the mirror appear smaller than they are*) traffic, and a high cost of living. But in actuality, we were running from a lack of support structure given our expanding family, and a lack of connection, or social network. We intrinsically knew that the way we were living was not right for us. What we found only appears to be toothless hillbillies in a town that just recently discovered fire. No, these are just the pixels in a bigger picture. I have no idea what that means, but it makes me sound educated and current.

Quite simply, we found exactly what we didn't know we were looking for: a greater sense of community, at a pace about three turns of the dial slower than that of a city.

When we first moved here, we were amazed by the sheer beauty of the Idaho Panhandle. Years later, we are amazed by the beauty of the people. Most of them, at least.

Acknowledgements:

About seven years ago, I got a call from a college friend I hadn't spoken to in at least 15 years prior. She implored me to write, based on our yearly Christmas letters. She continued this valued harassment for a few years thereafter. She read the very first, awful draft of this book, and thankfully is good-natured enough that she offered encouragement.

I would like to thank my editor, Lori Handelman, of Clear Voice Editing. Her deft, insightful comments and fierce protection of my voice made this an actual book: far better than what she initially encountered. I would also like to thank another beta reader, Phyllis Horvath, who despite what she read, offered encouragement. Finally, I would like to thank my family for giving me oodles of material and being good-natured about my exposing it. My sons, Austin, Jackson, and Sam are my joy. And my wife, Kim has been in my corner for many years. She is my rudder, my rock, and my best friend. To the moon and back.

The events in this book happened according to the author's addled memory. Names, descriptions and some locations have been changed to protect the innocent and guilty.